IS ME NOW
She

RECLAIM YOUR POWER, REWRITE YOUR STORY, & LIVE FULLY

From The Girl Who Was Lost…To the Woman Who Rose

BY: DR. MASHA LEKIC

Copyright © 2025 by DR. MASHA LEKIC
All Rights Reserved.

No part of this publication may be reproduced, stored in a retrieval system, or transmitted in any form or by any means — electronic, mechanical, photocopying, recording, or otherwise — without the prior written permission of the publisher, except for brief quotations used in reviews, articles, or academic work.

First Edition, 2025

ISBN:

Paperback: 978-1-917804-35-6
Hard Cover: 978-1-917804-36-3

Published by Gulf Publishers
www.gulfpublisher.com

Printed in United Arab Emirates.

This book is a work of non-fiction based on the author's lived experience. Any resemblance to real persons, living or dead, is purely coincidental unless explicitly stated.

TABLE OF CONTENTS

Dedications
About the Author
Introduction

**CHAPTER 1: Coming Home to Yourself –
Uncovering Who You Truly Are**   16

Who I Was   17
When My Body Forced Me to Wake Up   22
Unbecoming Everything You Are Not   25

**CHAPTER 2: The Love You Deserve – Rebuilding
Self-Worth & Inner Strength**   32

The Foundations of Self-Worth   33
Breaking the Cycle: From Self-Abandonment to Self-Respect   37
Embracing Solitude & Setting Standards for People   40

**CHAPTER 3: Learning To Live In The Now – No
More Someday**   49

The Fear of the Unknown   50
Releasing Mental Clutter & Emotional Baggage   54
Mastering Presence & Letting Go   57

Freeing Yourself from Punishment	127
Becoming Unbreakable	131
Choosing Yourself Every Day	134
Epilogue	**142**
Acknowledgments	**146**
Index	**150**

DEDICATIONS

To **Zoran, Matea, Leon** - my heart, my home. Your presence fills my life with purpose, and your love is my greatest treasure. You are the reason I keep moving forward, the force behind every lesson I have learned and every dream I refuse to give up on.

To **my beloved pets** - my healers, my little soulmates, who have given me unconditional love and comfort, reminding me of the purest form of connection and loving me without words. You saved me in a way that you will never know.

To **Shabbir & Branka** - my chosen family, my anchors in the world that often feel too heavy. The ones who have walked beside me through every storm. No matter the distance, no matter the challenges, I know you are always there - just as I am for you.

To **my parents** - my first teachers, my quiet strength, for shaping me in ways I only now begin to understand. To my father in heaven, always present, and to my mother, for what remains. For the strength, the sacrifices, and the journey that led me here.

To **the few who have remained** - your kindness, loyalty, and presence mean more than words can express. I see you, I appreciate you, and I am grateful for you.

To **those who did not believe in me**, who betrayed me, and who hurt me – thank you for revealing the truth I needed to see and showing me exactly who I never want to be.

ABOUT THE AUTHOR

Dr. Masha Lekic is a medical doctor with over 15 years of experience in cosmetic dermatology and anti-aging medicine. Her medical education and clinical training span Europe, the USA, and the UAE, where she earned two Master's degrees and a Doctorate in Medical Science — a foundation that fuels both her clinical work and her deep understanding of the mind-body connection and holistic healing.

Born in Serbia and now living in Dubai, Dr. Masha's life has been shaped by early adversity, unwavering discipline, and a devotion to truth — in both medicine and life. From surviving war to rebuilding her life from scratch and healing through chronic illness, her journey became the blueprint for everything she teaches today.

Her debut book reflects not just what she's studied, but what she's lived — a raw, honest exploration of self-worth, resilience, and personal transformation.

Today, Dr. Masha continues to inspire others through her clinical work, writing, yoga practice, and a healing philosophy rooted in authenticity, emotional strength, and integrated well-being. She is also a devoted advocate for animal welfare, and philanthropic efforts that support human and animal healing.

www.drmashalekic.com

@dr.mashalekic

INTRODUCTION
THE MOMENT EVERYTHING CHANGED

Life moves fast — faster than we notice, faster than we're prepared for. We spend so much of it looking ahead, convinced that everything we want is waiting in the future. Until one day, you look back and realize how much time has passed you by — and that you've been surviving more than you've been living. We get caught up in routines, responsibilities, and expectations, convinced that once we have more — more money, more success, more love — then we'll finally feel fulfilled.

But what if that's the biggest lie of all?

If success alone brought happiness, why do so many people who seem to have everything still feel lost? Still feel empty?

The truth is, abundance has never been about what we have — it's about who we are. It's about living in a way that reflects what truly matters, discovering a purpose that feels true to us, and standing fully in the truth of who we are without hiding or holding back.

I didn't learn this in moments of comfort. I learned it while surviving the things no child should ever have to endure. Not in peace, not in warmth — but in the cold reality of embargo and war, where strength wasn't a choice, it was the only way to stay alive.

I was born in Serbia, back when it was still part of Yugoslavia.

Childhood, for me, didn't mean playgrounds and bedtime stories — it meant war. The sound of NATO bombs wasn't distant or rare — it was daily, close enough to make the walls tremble. We were a constant target because of the bridge over the Danube River, just minutes from where I lived. Some nights, it felt like the earth might crack beneath us. Like the ground couldn't hold the weight of everything we were carrying. And the sky… it wasn't just above us, it was burning. I remember lying there in the dark, completely still, listening to every sound outside, not knowing if the next one would be the last… or if I'd ever open my eyes again.

There were no worm meals, no water, no electricity, no safety. Just hunger, desperation, and a cold that never left my bones. My body was weak — malnourished, exhausted — but I didn't have the luxury of breaking down. You don't get to break. You must keep going.

The damp shelter became my second home. Dark, cramped, and suffocating, it was the only place that felt somewhat safe. But no walls could shield me from the fear in my chest, the hunger that never left my stomach, or the constant uncertainty of tomorrow.

Even as everything else fell apart — the life I was born into, the stability I never knew, the safety every child deserves —I held on to the only thing they couldn't take from me: my mind. In the midst of it all, books became my escape, my lifeline, and my way out. I wasn't just trying to pass school — I was fighting for my future. Every lesson, every grade, every small achievement was a step toward something beyond war. Beyond fear.

And I didn't just aim to be a good student — I was the best student in my class. Because I had no other choice.

Looking back, I see how those years didn't just teach me how to survive — they gave me resilience, discipline , and the ability to keep going even when everything felt impossible.

Despite it all, I didn't just survive — I thrived. I went on to complete two universities, two master's degrees, and a doctorate. What started as a desperate attempt to escape my circumstances became a lifelong pursuit of excellence. My past shaped me, but it never defined me. Instead, it became the foundation for the person I was meant to be.

And yet, years later, I found myself standing in the middle of a life I had worked endlessly to build — accomplished, respected, and seemingly whole — but carrying a heaviness that I couldn't name. I had survived everything the world threw at me, but I had never stopped to ask what it cost me to stay so strong. That realization didn't come as a breakthrough. It came slowly, like a truth I had been avoiding. And it marked the beginning of everything that followed, not because something around me changed, but because I was finally ready to stop moving through life without presence and start living as myself.

Fifteen years ago, life brought me to Dubai, in the heart of the beautiful United Arab Emirates, and something inside me knew I was exactly where I was meant to be. It wasn't easy. In fact, it took years of perseverance, raising two children while building a new life from the ground up. But somehow, this city — the rhythm, the energy, the opportunity — became the only place on Earth I can truly call my home. Out of all the places I've ever been, Dubai embraced every version of me as I grew, healed, struggled, and transformed. I am beyond grateful for this city and this country. The UAE didn't just offer me a new beginning — it gave me a promising future.

That journey eventually led me to where I am today. I now work as a medical doctor specializing in cosmetic dermatology and aesthetic medicine, and I have the privilege of helping people feel more confident in their own skin. But over the years, I've learned something powerful — true transformation doesn't start on the outside. It starts deeper, in the parts of us no one else can see.

I see it every day — people hoping that fixing their reflection in the mirror will somehow fix something deeper inside. But no amount of treatments, no amount of external perfection, will ever fill the void of self-doubt, insecurity, or lack of self-worth. Real beauty, real confidence, real abundance — it all begins within.

And that's why I wrote this book.

"She Is Me Now: Reclaim Your Power, Rewrite Your Story & Live Fully" isn't just another self-help book. It's a blueprint for transformation. This isn't about just "thinking positively" or making minor lifestyle changes. It's about shifting the way you think, the way you see yourself, and reconnecting with who you truly are.

When we release the thoughts, fears, and old beliefs that no longer serve us, we create space for clarity, strength, and peace to return. We begin to hear ourselves again. Not the voice shaped by fear, but the one that's been waiting underneath it all to lead us forward.

This book will help you:

- Discover who you truly are and what you want in life
- Break free from limiting beliefs and self-sabotaging habits
- Build resilience and gain clarity when life feels heavy

- Strengthen your self-worth — inside and out
- Surround yourself with the right people and habits that elevate you
- Take back control of your time, your energy, and your life

This isn't about becoming someone new — it's about stepping into the most powerful version of you.

The Journey Begins Now

No matter where you are in your journey — whether you're just starting or ready for a deeper shift — this book will meet you where you are. Each chapter will push you to rethink what you believe, unlearn what no longer serves you, and take real, meaningful steps toward a life of confidence, purpose, and freedom .

And if you ever doubt whether you can do this, remember this: I am proof that you can.

You don't need permission to take back control of your life.

You don't need validation to make different choices.

You don't need to wait for the right moment.

You just need to remember that your life still belongs to you.

And it's not too late to begin again — on your terms, in your way, for your own peace.

So let's begin — not with perfection, but with truth.

Not with who you were expected to be, but with the version of you that's always been waiting — powerful, whole, and finally free.

CHAPTER: 01

COMING HOME TO YOURSELF – UNCOVERING WHO YOU TRULY ARE

Who I Was

From the moment we are born, life begins shaping us. Expectations come at us from every direction — from family, culture, and society. Long before we even begin to figure out who we truly are, we learn who we are supposed to be.

We are told to be kind, to be strong, to succeed. And so, we adapt.

We push ourselves to be the best — the best son or daughter, the best student, the best friend, the best partner, the best professional. We chase perfection, not because it makes us happy, but because we believe that's what makes us worthy. We become masters at meeting everyone else's expectations. But at what cost?

I lived this way for years.

I was the student who never allowed herself to fail, who pushed harder than anyone else, who believed her worth was tied to her success. I graduated with top honors, but none of it came easily. It was built on sleepless nights, relentless pressure, and an unshakable fear that it wasn't good enough.

I wasn't just studying — I was fighting for perfection. I wasn't satisfied with simply understanding a subject; I needed to know every detail, down to the smallest thing. Every exam felt like a battle I had to win. I gave up sleep, convinced that resting meant failing — and failure was not an option.

Looking back now, I realize how exhausted I was. But at that time, I thought exhaustion was normal. No matter how much I achieved, it never felt like enough. Every perfect grade gave me relief for a moment, but soon after, there was always a new challenge waiting. I was never competing with anyone else — I was fighting myself. Fighting the impossible standards I had created.

The pressure I put on myself was suffocating. I loved learning — I still do — but somewhere along the way, my achievements stopped feeling like my own. The more I accomplished, the more I felt disconnect ed from who I really was.

I was also the daughter who never disappointed. The one who carried responsibilities in silence, fulfilling every role with discipline and care. I learned very young that being "good" meant being responsible.

I was just nine years old when I began cooking meals for my family and baking desserts. I still remember how small I was, barely able to reach the kitchen counter. My mother would put a chair beneath my feet so I could stir the pot or wash the dishes.

But cooking wasn't just about helping out — it was survival.

The war had taken away so much from us. There was no abundance, only scarcity. I learned how to make something out of nothing. Flour, water, and a pinch of salt became bread. A single potato had to be enough for the whole family. I stirred soups made from almost nothing, watching my mother ration every bite so we would have enough for the next day.

At the time, I didn't think of it as a hardship. It was simply life. But now, when I look back, I see how much that tiny girl carried on her shoulders. How early I learned to take care of others before even understanding what it meant to care for myself.

Cleaning the entire house was part of my routine, too. Scrubbing floors, dusting every shelf, and making sure everything was perfect. We couldn't afford help, so I felt like it was my job. Both my parents were working hard to keep us afloat, and I wanted to do my part. In all those silent sacrifices, I never once asked myself what it was that I truly wanted.

I was also the friend who was always there. The one who gave more than she received. The one who made sure everyone else was okay, even when I wasn't. I shaped myself into whoever people needed me to be. I listened, supported, and showed up.

I ignored my own needs, my own dreams, my own voice. And for what?

I spent decades suffering for people who only took from me. People who had their own selfish needs, their hidden agendas, and their own unspoken motives. I wanted to believe in kindness and loyalty. I wanted to believe that people would love me for who I was. But life taught me otherwise.

I learned the hard way that most people stay only as long as they can benefit from you. Their kindness has limits. Their loyalty has an expiration date. And when you have nothing left to give, they leave without a second thought.

The deepest betrayals didn't come from strangers — they came from those I trusted most.

A family friend — someone I had known since childhood, someone who had been like family — abandoned me when I needed him most. Someone I would have defended with my life, who I had stood by unconditionally, turned his back on me the moment caring became inconvenient.

That kind of betrayal doesn't just hurt — it breaks something inside you. It makes you question everything.

And then, there was the one I called my best friend for two decades. We shared everything — dreams, fears, memories. I believed she would be there for me, no matter what. But in the end, she was no different from the others. The pain of losing her was unlike anything I could describe. To invest so much of yourself into someone, only to realize they never valued you the same way — that wound runs deep.

For years, I excused people's awful behavior. I told myself that if I loved them harder, if I gave more, they would change. I was afraid to lose them. Afraid to be alone. Afraid to admit that some people will never truly care.

I tolerated things I should never have accepted. I endured wounds that no one should ever have to bear. All because I believed that love, friendship, and family were worth suffering for.

But I was wrong.

Now, I see it clearly: people will take from you as long as you let them. They will drain you if you allow it. They will always choose themselves first. And when you have nothing left, they'll walk away — without guilt, without regret.

In the end, I was left with nothing but the truth: most people only care when it serves them.

I was also the partner who loved deeply but lost herself completely. In my teenage years, I poured everything I had into a few relationships, thinking that love was about putting others first. I stayed in situations that broke me, believing that if I was patient and loving enough, I would be chosen, I would be enough.

But how could I expect someone to choose me when I hadn't even chosen myself?

I learned that, for many, love is about convenience — about what they can get. People don't love — they use. They take what they need — attention, validation, pleasure — and when they're done, they move on. No explanation. No care for what they've left behind. They say the right words — promises of forever — and vanish when things get real.

I watched as men clung to me when they needed something and disappeared when love required effort. I saw people swap partners like changing clothes, pretending it was love when all it was… was need.

For years, I believed in fairy tales. I believed love would be strong enough to overcome anything. But life showed me that many people are incapable of real love.

And that realization broke my heart, but it also set me free.

I was also the professional who gave her all, sacrificing sleep, health, and peace just to succeed. I worked myself to exhaustion, believing that success had to come through suffering. I thought slowing down meant failing.

I gave my all — my skill, knowledge, discipline — believing that dedication would be recognized. But instead, I was met with betrayal, disrespect, and lies. I watched people play dirty games to climb the ladder, while those of us who worked hard and honestly were taken for granted. I endured numerous delayed or not paid salaries, empty promises, and toxic environments where I was only valued for what I could give, not for who I was.

And in all of this, I became everything I was expected to be.

But in doing so, I lost myself.

When My Body Forced Me to Wake Up

For as long as I can remember, I've been struggling with various health issues — some visible, others hidden so well that only a few people ever knew. These weren't just difficult moments that would eventually pass. It felt like a never-ending cycle — one issue after another, and every time, I told myself to just keep going, to keep pushing through, as if being strong enough could somehow make it all disappear.

But every symptom, every setback, every diagnosis was bringing me closer to breaking.

I've always been disciplined, resilient, and driven. Yet no success could quiet what my body was trying to tell me.

Since childhood, illness has been my constant companion. I spent years in and out of clinics and hospitals, surrounded by surgeries, tests, and endless questions no one could answer. I can still remember sitting in sterile hospital rooms, surrounded by the sharp smell of disinfectants, listening to machines beeping through the night.

I was carrying the weight of a body that felt like it was fighting itself. An immune system that failed me. A digestive system that never healed. A spine that ached under the pressure of always pushing too hard.

Day after day, year after year, the suffering was unbearable. Chronic pain that stole my sleep. A fatigue so heavy that no rest could fix it. The discomfort was so overwhelming, and even the simplest tasks felt too much.

Still, I didn't listen.

I pushed my body to its edge, thinking inner strength alone could overpower what was breaking inside. I told myself that if I worked harder, disciplined myself more, and ignored the pain long enough, maybe I could make it all go away.

But my body was done waiting, and it started shutting down. Bit by bit — it began to withdraw because I had asked too much of it for too long. It wasn't just physical pain anymore. It was years of emotional pressure I never released. Years of pushing through without pausing. Years of showing up for everything and everyone — but not for myself.

Because this wasn't just about being sick — it was something much deeper. My body was carrying everything I refused to feel. The stress I silenced. The anger I swallowed. The heartbreak I buried. And it had reached a point where it couldn't carry it anymore. Even though I ignored it for years, there comes a point when you can't pretend anymore.

For me, that moment came through my body.

It was no longer just stress, no longer just tiredness, no longer just discomfort.

It was a situation of life or death.

Some days, the pain was so overwhelming that moving felt impossible. And there were nights when I lay wide awake, staring at the ceiling, asking myself if I would ever feel whole again. Mornings didn't make it easier. They only reminded me of how much strength it would take just to make it through another day. Even breathing felt like a fight — a quiet struggle between holding on and giving up.

Doctors kept searching for answers, but deep down, I already knew what they couldn't see.

My body was begging me to stop, to listen, and to finally wake up.

It felt like it was giving up on me, but the truth was, I had abandoned it long before it started breaking down.

For years, I refused to see the warning signs. I kept telling myself that suffering was part of life. But denial only gets you so far. Because you can't abandon yourself and expect to thrive.

The wake-up call was brutal. I had no choice but to face it. If I didn't change, my body wouldn't hold on much longer. And that terrified me. Because if I weren't the strong, unstoppable, disciplined woman I had spent years building, then who was I? But my body, in the end, became my greatest teacher.

Every illness, every sleepless night, every moment of pain — none of it was random. It was the only language my body had left to get my attention. It had tried everything — fatigue, tension, discomfort – and when I did not listen, it forced me to stop the only way it could: by making it impossible to go on the way I used to.

It wasn't just a struggle to overcome — it was a message. A wake-up call. A choice.

To keep breaking myself for the sake of some illusion.

Or to stop, listen, and finally come home for myself.

Unbecoming Everything You Are Not

There comes a moment when you realize that the person you've been is not the person you were ever meant to be.

Not because you were weak. Not because you failed. But because, for so long, you carried a version of yourself that was built to survive, not to live your truth. Not to feel joy. Not to feel peace. A version shaped by expectations, by duty, by the silent rules of a world that defined you before you ever had the chance to ask: "Who am I?"

This journey isn't about becoming someone new.

It's about letting go of everything you are not.

It's about peeling back the layers of conditioning that told you who you needed to be to belong. The labels, the roles, the rules. The ways you betrayed yourself to fit in — choices that seemed small at the time but eventually became the walls of a life that no longer feels like your own.

Unbecoming isn't gentle. It's not neat, easy, or comfortable.

It's standing in front of the mirror and seeing — maybe for the first time — the weight of a life shaped by everyone else's expectations. It's realizing how much of yourself you've silenced just to avoid conflict. It's the ache of stepping out of identities that once made you feel safe but now suffocate you. It's grieving the version of yourself that tried so hard to do everything right — who followed the path, obeyed the rules, made sacrifice after sacrifice — only to realize that none of it gave you what you truly longed for. And you wonder if anyone ever really saw you or if they just loved the version of you who always held it together, no matter how much it cost.

It's terrifying to walk away from what you've always known. To stop being the person others expect you to be. To speak up when you used to stay quiet. To take the space where you used to make yourself small. To step into the unknown without the mask you've worn for years. It shakes everything you thought you were standing on, leaving you to question who you really are when you're no longer shaped by what others expect of you.

And then you have to face the hardest question — if not this, then what? A life of quiet resentment? A life where you keep folding yourself smaller, bending and twisting just to be accepted? A life that looks polished on the outside but feels empty and cold on the inside?

Because that's what happens when you keep carrying what was never meant for you. That's what happens when your truth is always the first thing you sacrifice.

But when you finally stop pretending — when you let go of everything that was never truly yours — something inside of you shifts. The noise fades. The weight lifts. And in that stillness, you begin to hear your own voice again.

Not the voice shaped by fear, or pressure, or expectations. But the voice that has been waiting all along for you to return. The one that remembers who you were before the roles, before the pressure, before the pleasing.

At first, it feels strange. Almost like meeting a stranger. Because when you've spent a lifetime adjusting yourself to fit into what the world wants, being real can feel like unfamiliar ground. It is uncertain, but it is yours. And for the first time, you start to feel like you belong–not to others, but to yourself.

With every step forward, with every truth spoken, with every moment you choose yourself over the illusion of acceptance, you start to remember.

You were never meant to be anyone but yourself.

And this world doesn't need another perfect person.

It needs someone real.

THE SHIFT

This Is Who I Am Now

Take ten minutes today to be with yourself. Not to plan, not to fix anything — just to sit with the version of you that has spent years trying to be enough for everyone else. Bring with you only a blank sheet of paper and a pen — something clear and real, something that lets you put into words what you've never had the space or permission to say.

Begin by writing down every name, title, expectation, and moment that ever made you believe that your truth was inconvenient. Think of the ways you were told to behave — how you were expected to speak, to look, to succeed, to stay small, to not take up too much space. Think of the situations where you felt you had to hold back who you really were in order to keep the peace or avoid judgment. Let all of it come out. You don't need to get it right — you just need to be honest.

Once it's all on the page, draw a box around what you've written. Not to contain it, but to separate it from yourself. Give it a name. Call it:

"What I've outgrown."

Then, turn the page.

Start again with this sentence:

"If I didn't care what anyone expected, this is who I'd be…"

Write one paragraph. Or more if something inside wants to keep going. Don't overthink it. Don't try to explain or defend what comes out. Just write from the part of you that knows exactly how you want to live — without filters, without hesitation.

When you finish, fold the paper and keep it somewhere personal. You don't need to reread it often. Just know it's there. What you wrote isn't just a reflection — it's a decision. A moment you stopped carrying what never felt like yours and started choosing what actually does.

Let that page remind you of what's real. Not who you were expected to be, but who you already are.

And if one day you feel uncertain again, go back to it — not for answers, but to remember that you already told the truth.

This is who I am now. And that's enough.

She is no longer breaking. She is becoming.

CHAPTER: 02

The Love You Deserve – Rebuilding Self-Worth & Inner Strength

The Foundations of Self-Worth

I used to believe that love was something you had to earn. You had to prove yourself worthy of it, mold yourself into something lovable, achieve enough, be enough, and give enough. But love was never meant to be a reward. It's not a medal for perfect behavior or a prize handed out when we become someone else's version of "good enough." Love is something we're born deserving of. Something that lives inside us, even when life tries its hardest to make us forget it was ever there.

Still, we spend years looking for it in all the wrong places — in achievements, in people, in perfection. Especially when love, in our early years, was distant or given only in pieces. When it was absent, unpredictable, or wrapped in conditions, it shaped the way we saw ourselves. It created patterns — like chasing approvals, molding ourselves to meet expectations, or giving so much in hopes that one day, maybe, we'd finally be "enough."

As a child, I carried an emptiness I couldn't name. Was it the war that tore through our lives? Was it the nights I lay awake listening to sirens, unsure if we'd make it until morning? The instability, the fear, the unknown? Was it my parents — two people worn down by holding everything together, their love buried beneath the silence — struggling under the weight of survival, with no space left for affection? Or maybe it was the unspoken responsibilities I was too young to carry and understand?

I had an older sister. Our relationship was often tense and filled with conflict — two children surviving under pressure, without the space to be soft with one another. But even then, her presence shaped those years. Our grandmother lived with us, and despite everything, she became a source of comfort. In a world that rarely felt safe, her presence gave me small moments of steadiness — something my heart held onto, even when nothing else made sense.

Love felt like something I could see but never touch. Always just out of reach. Something I believed I had to fight for. To prove I was worthy of.

The environment I grew up in was strict. Everything had to be in order — perfectly timed, perfectly done. Mistakes weren't gently corrected; they were pointed out with weight and shouting. There was no softness. No space to be messy, to be unsure, to just be. Every move was calculated. Every moment was monitored. I lived in a constant state of vigilance — aware of time, aware of consequences, and terrified of letting anyone down.

And yet, I don't blame my parents. They did the best they could with what they had in a world that gave them no kindness. But still, in that process, love slowly turned into something that felt more like responsibility than connection. It turned into a duty. Into something heavy, something expected, rather than something felt.

Deep down, I longed for something else. For warmth, for softness, for shared moments — not built on hardship, but on connection. I wanted to sit with my family at a restaurant, enjoying the food, but not checking the prices. I wanted to wake up on Christmas morning to joy, to traditions, to safety. I wanted spontaneous family vacations that would create lifelong memories. I wanted hugs that lasted more than a second, someone noticing when I was breaking down. I longed for bedtime stories, not just survival plans. For someone to tell me they were proud of me, not just when I succeeded, but when I was simply me. But those moments were rare. And as the war stole away what was left of my childhood, they faded into distant moments I still ache for.

School became my escape — but it also became my prison. Being the best student wasn't something that brought admiration. It brought resentment. I was called the "nerd," the one who always knew the answers. But inside? I was lonely. Friendships were hard to build, even harder to trust.

In my teenage years, I tried to fill that void in a few relationships, hoping someone else could finally fill what I couldn't name. I thought that maybe — if someone loved me enough — it would fix the emptiness I carried. But instead of love, I found more pain. Those relationships were unhealthy, leaving me feeling lonelier than before.

And all of that – the emptiness, the striving, the pain — followed me into adulthood. I tied my worth to what I could achieve. I was proud of my discipline, of how much I could push myself, of never giving up. I became the woman who could do it all. The woman who carried everything and everyone. But I also see now how much of it came from a place of proving. Of trying to earn what I didn't believe I already deserved.

Because there's a difference between self-esteem and self-worth. Self-esteem is knowing what we're capable of. But self-worth ? That's knowing we're valuable even when we have nothing to show for it.

I didn't understand that back then.

So I shrank to fit expectations. I stayed quiet when I should have spoken. I gave when I had nothing left. I remained in places I had outgrown. In relationships that no longer served me. In roles that drained me. I stayed where I wasn't seen, where I wasn't appreciated. Not because I didn't know better, but because I hadn't yet learned that I didn't have to earn my worth.

Low self-worth doesn't always come with obvious signs. Sometimes it's hidden in the ways we second-guess ourselves before speaking. In how we tolerate the things that hurt us, just to keep the peace. It shows up in the way we let people treat us. In the way we hesitate to set boundaries . It's when we stay that we know we should leave. In the way we tell ourselves: *"Maybe this is all I deserve."*

It affects everything — our choices, our relationships, our careers, and our mental health. Because when we don't believe we deserve more, we stop reaching for it.

But I'm not that person anymore.

Learning to say "no" became my superpower.

Walking away from people who drained me became my freedom.

Choosing myself over and over again became the greatest act of love I've ever known.

Because self-worth is not something another person hands you. It's not given by parents, by partners, or by friends. It's something you reclaim, piece by piece, every time you decide not to abandon yourself.

And when you do — when you finally stand in that truth, your own value, your own heart — you realize the love you've been searching for has always been inside of you.

Breaking the Cycle: From Self-Abandonment to Self-Respect

I reached a point in my life when I could no longer pretend that everything was fine. The weight of constantly putting others first — of meeting expectations that were never truly mine to carry—became too heavy. Somewhere along the way, I stopped recognizing myself. I spent so long being who I thought I needed to be that I forgot to ask myself if there was anything left of me beneath it all.

My body gave out before my mind did. When my health broke down, to the point where I had no choice but to face the truth, I finally saw what I had been running from for years — I had abandoned myself. I had been so focused on holding everything together that I didn't even realize how far I'd gone from my own truth, my own limits, my own abilities. I stopped checking in with myself. I stopped asking what I needed. I just kept going.

I had spent so much time making sure everyone else was okay. Fulfilling responsibilities. Living up to what others wanted from me. But I neglected the one responsibility that mattered most — myself.

I was always pushing, always enduring, always giving — until I reached a place where there was no way back. And when I hit rock bottom, when there was nothing left to hold onto, I saw my life with painful clarity:

I had a choice — I could keep walking down that path and lose myself completely.

Or I could make a promise — A promise that I would never, ever abandon myself again.

Self-abandonment doesn't always look like falling apart. Sometimes, it hides behind responsibility and routine. It convinces you that putting yourself last means you care, that ignoring your own needs is love, and that silencing your desires is the price you have to pay to be accepted. It happens when you quiet your intuition to avoid conflict. When you keep going, even when your body begs you to stop, because people count on you. When you become whoever others need you to be, just to fit someone else's comfort.

Until one day, you look around and don't recognize the life you're in or the person you've become.

Self-abandonment shows up most painfully in love. So many people, including myself, have been trapped in that cycle, especially in relationships . Believing that love would complete us, fix us, and save us. We believe that if we give enough and sacrifice enough, someone will finally fill that empty space inside. But I've learned that attachment is not love. Habit is not love. Tolerating less than you deserve just to avoid being alone — that is not love.

And it always goes back to where it began — in our childhood . Our early wounds shape everything. The way we see ourselves. What we think we deserve. For me, the pain I carried as a child, the feeling of not being seen, not being understood, always needing to prove my worth — followed me into adulthood like an invisible thread I couldn't cut.

The choices I made, the people I let into my life, the way I handed my happiness over to others — it all came from wounds that were still wide open.

Without realizing it, I kept repeating what felt familiar, because even unhealthy love feels "safe" when it's all you've ever known. I made choices I wish I hadn't, not because I was weak, but because I was hurting.

Healing isn't about blaming the past. It's about breaking free from it. It's about realizing that, yes, the pain we carry may not be our fault, but healing it is our responsibility. And healing doesn't come from someone else. It doesn't come from the love we keep begging for. It comes from within. Because no one can complete us. No one can give us the love we've been denying ourselves. The work is ours to do.

So that's what I did.

Step by step, I started to honor myself in ways I never had before. I started listening – really listening. To that small voice inside — the one I had ignored for so long. I began trusting my own intuition because every time I went against it, I paid the price. I stopped justifying why I deserved better. I stopped explaining myself to people who were never meant to understand me. I made choices that felt right for me, not choices driven by fear or guilt. I stopped giving my energy to people, places, and things that were bad for my mental health.

To anything that required me to betray myself just to be accepted.

And for the first time, my life felt like it was mine. Not a duty. But something real. Something I could fully live and breathe.

Most of all, I learned that self-respect isn't just about setting boundaries with others. It's also about setting boundaries with yourself. It's about refusing to tolerate your own self-destructive patterns. Choosing your well-being over temporary comfort. Standing up for yourself — even when no one else does. Fighting for your peace — the peace that had been lost for too long.

And the most beautiful thing is this — the moment you reclaim your power, the moment you stop settling for less than you deserve, everything begins to shift.

The right people start to show up.

The right doors begin to open.

Life starts to meet you where you are.

Because you were never meant to stay small. You were never meant to shrink yourself just to make others more comfortable, or to live a life built around everyone else's needs.

You're here to take up space.

To honor your needs.

To finally live on your terms, for you.

Embracing Solitude & Setting Standards for People

Some of the most profound transformations happen in solitude. It's in those silent moments — when there are no distractions and no noise from the outside world — that you finally begin to meet yourself. You start learning how to love yourself, not just on the surface, but deep within, in the most honest and raw parts of who you are. You learn to sit with your thoughts, your fears, your dreams, and your pain, and instead of running from them, you begin to hold space for them.

When you reach that place, you discover a kind of wisdom that only stillness can offer — a wisdom that cannot be found in the noise of others' opinions but only in the silence of your own heart. Because solitude isn't loneliness — it's self-discovery, clarity, and a kind of freedom that only comes when you no longer need anyone else to tell you who you are.

When you are truly at peace within yourself, you stop accepting half-hearted efforts and conditional love. You stop shrinking yourself just to be accepted. You no longer settle for people who treat you like an option because, deep inside, you know you were never meant to be one. You were meant to be a priority. You were meant to be loved fully, not in pieces.

And something incredible happens when you realize that being alone isn't a weakness — but one of your greatest strengths.

Because when you no longer fear being alone, you become untouchable. You become whole on your own, and no one can take that away from you.

Solitude gives you the space to pause and reflect. To look inward and ask: *"What do I really want? What do I need? What have I been accepting that no longer serves me?"* It helps you understand your dreams and values , and what truly fulfills you, instead of what merely fills an empty space. It teaches you to see the difference between what feels right for your soul and what only serves as a temporary distraction from loneliness.

In stillness, you grow strong enough to stand by your choices, even when others don't understand them. Even when they question you. Because you begin to trust that your intuition knows the way.

But choosing solitude doesn't mean building walls. It means creating doors that open only for those who bring real value, kindness, and respect into your life. It's no longer about proving your worth to people who cannot see it. It's about cultivating relationships that nourish you — that add meaning and depth, not ones that leave you feeling empty and drained. And above all else, it's about building a relationship with yourself — the one person you will always have, no matter what.

Still, I know that for many, solitude feels like a scary place. The fear of being alone keeps so many people stuck in relationships that don't nourish them. They settle for being half-loved, for being tolerated instead of cherished, because the idea of walking alone feels harder than staying where they are. But here's what I've learned: Solitude is not the absence of others. It's the presence of self. It's being so connected to your own soul that you no longer fear the empty spaces. When you embrace it, you find a peace that is so deep. You realize that you are whole and complete, just as you are.

Your entire life starts to shift the moment you set standards that are rooted in deep self-respect . When you stop tolerating inconsistency — when you finally say: "I am not available for anything less than I deserve." When you no longer entertain people who make you feel like you must prove your worth to be loved.

Because love is never something you should have to earn.

People who drain you, who don't show up, who make you question your own value — they no longer deserve a place in your life.

And the most powerful truth is this:

You don't owe anyone an explanation for wanting more.

You don't need to explain to anyone why you deserve to be treated with care, respect, and consistency.

Your worth is not up for negotiation.

The people who cannot meet you where you are — who cannot rise to meet your standards — will naturally fall away.

And that is not a loss. That is alignment with who you truly are.

Setting standards is never about arrogance. It's not superiority. It's about self-preservation. It's about knowing that your time, energy, love, and presence are sacred, and not everyone deserves access to them. It's about honoring yourself enough to walk away from anything that feels small, anything that makes you shrink.

You deserve deep, meaningful connections.

You deserve conversations that light up your soul, not ones that drain you.

You deserve to be met with love that is consistent, kind, and real, not love that comes and goes, leaving you anxious and questioning yourself.

You deserve people who respect your boundaries, who respect your heart, not people who take and take until there is nothing left.

And this transformation — this stepping into your power — doesn't always happen easily. Sometimes, it happens in small but important decisions.

You start choosing differently, not out of bitterness, but out of wisdom.

You stop chasing — you start attracting.

You stop begging — you start walking away.

And when you do that, you create room for people who respect you, who value you, who love you without conditions — people who show up in action, not just empty words.

The moment you find peace in solitude and stop lowering your standards, you take your power back. You step into a life where you no longer ask for permission to be respected — you simply embody it.

It's the moment when you realize that you are already enough.

You are already whole.

And anyone who cannot see that was never meant to walk beside you.

THE SHIFT

The Wholeness Test

If you want to know where your self-worth was fractured, look at the moments you started hiding the parts of you that felt "too much." Not because they were — but because someone made you believe they were.

Maybe it started in childhood when your needs made someone uncomfortable, and instead of care, you received distance. Maybe it was in a relationship where the love you gave was never returned with the same depth, and so you began to shape yourself into someone more palatable. Or maybe it's now — in a life that looks stable on the outside but slowly erodes you every time you put yourself last just to keep things together.

This is how it happens. We don't wake up one day believing we're unworthy. We arrive there slowly, by surviving moments where we had to choose between being honest and being accepted.

And because survival always wins, we learn to wear the version of ourselves that gets the least rejection — the one who stays silent, keeps giving, never asks for too much, and never needs too often.

But the truth is: that version isn't loved — it's tolerated. And deep down, you've always known that.

Now, try this:

Before you fall asleep tonight, lie down with your body fully supported. One hand on your heart, one on your stomach. Breathe in through your nose and out through your mouth — slowly, fully, without force. Let your system settle.

Ask yourself, gently and without needing answers:

Where am I still carrying the belief that I have to be easy, quiet, or selfless to be worthy of love?

Feel for it — not in your thoughts, but in your body. Where does it tighten? Where does it ache? Where does it pull?

And then say — softly, so your body hears it:

"I no longer carry the shape they needed me to become. I don't have to shrink just to be seen."

Stay with that truth. Let it stretch out inside you. Let it breathe. Let it take up space in places where silence once lived.

This isn't about becoming someone new.

It's about no longer abandoning who you were before the world taught you to be smaller to stay loved.

She unchained herself from the past – Her self-worth and true love began the moment her self-abandonment ended.

CHAPTER: 03

Learning To Live In The Now – No More Someday

The Fear of the Unknown

I've spent so much of my life waiting.

Waiting to feel ready. Waiting for the right moment. Waiting for life to give me permission to finally start living fully, as if someone had to give me approval.

I used to believe that day would come — the day when everything would magically fall into place. When I'd wake up with clarity, knowing exactly what to do. When all the doubts would disappear. When I would suddenly become fearless enough to choose what I really wanted, and what set my soul on fire.

But that day? It never came.

Instead, I kept holding my breath, watching life move on around me while I stood on the sidelines of my own dreams. "Not now. Not yet. Maybe later," I kept telling myself. And without even realizing it, I was putting off my happiness — again and again, like I wasn't allowed to live it yet, like my life wasn't quite ready to be lived.

I saved beautiful dresses for occasions that never happened. They stayed hidden in my closet like fragile pieces of a life I was too scared to live. I kept ideas locked away inside my head — book titles, projects, dreams — waiting for some perfect, polished version of me — the one who would one day feel worthy enough to bring them to life. I passed by thousands of restaurants I wanted to try, skipped invitations I would've loved to say yes to, and declined adventures that whispered life into my spirit. All because I believed I had to earn them first — earn joy, earn rest, earn peace.

But it wasn't just the dreams, ideas, and dresses.

I was holding back my own voice — my opinions, my emotions, my needs — like they were too loud, too much, too inconvenient. I swallowed my truth more times than I can count, not because it wasn't real, but because I didn't believe I was allowed to take up that kind of space.

And beautiful trips I longed for — the ones I knew would heal me, inspire me, breathe life back into my soul — stayed as nothing more than distant daydreams. I kept whispering to myself: *"When I have more money. When I have more time. When I'm ready."*

But the truth is, while I was waiting for life to become perfect, life was quietly passing by me.

I postponed laughter. I postponed joy. I even delayed peace, as if all of it belonged to a future version of me who had proven herself enough to finally deserve it.

Looking back, I know I was afraid. Afraid to live before I was "ready". Afraid to want too much and be disappointed. Afraid to lose what I hadn't even allowed myself to experience yet. So I stayed in the waiting while aching to breathe, to feel alive, to stop holding back.

But life has a way of showing us that time doesn't wait for us to be ready.

It took some of the hardest, most devastating moments of my life — moments that broke me open in ways I never thought possible — to finally understand this truth: there is no perfect time to begin.

There's only right now, and all the time I spent waiting was time I could never get back.

A deeply transformative shift in my mindset happened during my yoga teacher training.

At first, I enrolled in the course because of my passion for movement and self-discipline . But what I found was something much greater. In one of our first classes, the teacher said something that stayed with me, even when I wanted to resist it. The ancient teaching of yoga held a wisdom so profound and yet so simple:

"All that exists is this moment."

At first, my mind pushed against that. I was used to planning, controlling, analyzing, and always thinking five steps ahead. But little by little, I realized how much of my life I had spent in every place but here.

Living in memories and in fear of the future.

But not living in the actual moment I was in.

And when I finally started to notice — when I really paid attention — I saw all the tiny miracles that I had been missing.

I started noticing the small moments I once ignored — the way morning light softly fills my room as I open my eyes. The sacred stillness before the world rises. The comforting ritual of wrapping my hands around a warm cup of morning tea. The kind of laughter that makes your body forget its pain. The sound of my cat purring on my lap. The familiar scent of my home after a long day.

I began to see that life isn't something that waits for us. It's not sitting in the future, waiting for us to "deserve" it. Life is happening now — in all these moments we overlook because we're too busy waiting for something bigger.

So I stopped waiting, because life won't wait for me.

The past? It's gone. No amount of thinking will rewrite it.

The future? It's unknown. No matter how much we plan, we don't control it.

But here, now — this is all we truly have.

When I finally let that sink in, it broke my heart — for all the days I had lost waiting to be "enough." But it also woke me up. I stopped saving my life for later. I stopped telling myself that joy belongs to some future version of me.

Instead, I started living inside the life I already had — in all its messiness, its perfect imperfections, in all its uncertainty, in all its small, breathtaking moments. Because this moment — the one you and I are in right now — is the only one we know for sure we have.

And if there's one thing I've learned, it's this: you don't have to have it all figured out to start living. You don't have to be "ready." You just have to be here.

So maybe, if you've been waiting — for the right time, for the right version of you — I hope you'll remember this:

Sometimes, the bravest thing you can do is start living before you feel ready.

Because life is happening now. And you are allowed to live it fully, freely, on your terms.

Releasing Mental Clutter & Emotional Baggage

We carry so much more than we realize — not just the weight of our physical responsibilities but also the invisible burdens of unresolved emotions, past regrets, and beliefs that no longer serve us. Our minds accumulate layers of thoughts and emotions, some of which are deeply embedded, making it difficult to fully live in the present moment. The more we hold on to the past, the more we lose our ability to be truly engaged in the now.

Imagine your mind as a room filled with objects — memories, worries, and fears. When there's too much in it, it's hard to move through it, to breathe, or even notice what's right in front of you. We end up bumping into old pain, tripping over things we thought we'd already let go of, squeezing past the clutter of doubt we never meant to keep.

This is what happens when we refuse to let go when we convince ourselves that every experience, every wound, must remain a permanent fixture in our minds. But what if we chose to declutter? What if we consciously removed what no longer serves us and made room for something new?

Some burdens have been with us for so long that they feel like part of our identity. I know this firsthand.

Growing up under the weight of war and almost a decade of sanctions and embargoes, I learned to carry pain before I could even understand what it was. And for years, I didn't even recognize the weight I was carrying. The fear, the anxiety, the need to analyze every situation to anticipate danger — it became second nature to me. And even though life has moved forward, sometimes it feels like the echoes of those early experiences are still with me, shaping how I process emotions, how I see the world, and how I hold on to things that I should have let go of long ago.

We often don't realize how much weight we are carrying until we feel the heaviness becomes unbearable, not just in our bodies, but in our minds and in our spirit. We wonder why we feel drained, unmotivated, or unable to fully embrace joy. But the answer is simple: we are too full of the past to receive the present.

Consider the pain of betrayal — a relationship where trust was broken, a friendship that ended abruptly, or a childhood wound that never fully healed. These experiences shape the way we interact with the world today. And if left unchecked, they become the lens through which we see life, distorting our ability to trust, love, and be open to new experiences.

Much of our mental clutter comes from trying to control the uncontrollable. We analyze endlessly — conversations, decisions, relationships, events, even the smallest details — believing that if we can anticipate every possible outcome, we can somehow protect ourselves from pain or disappointment. We carry the weight of "what ifs" and "should haves", replaying past mistakes and trying to predict future challenges — as if overthinking could grant us certainty. But it never does. The past cannot be rewritten, and the future will always be a mystery. The only thing we ever truly own in this life — is this moment.

There is a reason why the mind clings to pain, why it struggles to release old wounds. It believes that by holding on, it can make sense of what happened — that if we just understand it enough, maybe it won't hurt so much. But the truth is, understanding does not heal — letting go does. We do not need to solve every mystery of our past to move forward. Sometimes, we need to make peace with the fact that some things will never make sense — and that's okay. Healing doesn't come from figuring everything out perfectly; it comes from deciding that the past won't control our future anymore.

Letting go of emotional baggage is an act of gaining your inner peace back. It's choosing to no longer be defined by what hurt us. It's looking at the fears and patterns we've inherited, not with judgment, but with compassion, and then choosing to step beyond them. It's allowing stillness to enter our minds, creating space for beauty and clarity to grow.

To live in the now isn't just to be present — it's to be fully available to life. It's to walk without the extra weight, to breathe without yesterday pressing against your ribs. It's to wake up and see the world not as a projection of past wounds but as it truly is — a vast, open space of possibilities.

When we release mental clutter and emotional baggage, we make space. We stop surviving, and we start living.

And in that space, peace, clarity, and a sense of calm begin to take root.

Mastering Presence & Letting Go

Life is happening now — not in the past you keep revisiting, nor in the future you anxiously anticipate. It unfolds only in this moment — in the space between your inhalation and exhalation, between your thoughts and awareness. Yet, so many of us exist anywhere but here, tangled in regret or chasing what's next, always believing fulfillment is just out of reach.

But presence isn't something we achieve. It's something we return to when we finally stop running. It doesn't need to be mastered; it just needs to be felt. And often, we miss it because we've been taught to value movement over stillness, noise over silence, doing over simply being. The more we slow down, the more we see that presence was never gone — we were just too far away from ourselves to notice. The mind, by its nature, is restless. It clings to memories, constructs endless possibilities, and holds tightly to anything that gives it a sense of security. This is why letting go feels so unnatural sometimes. We are wired to cling to people, to beliefs, to identities - even when they no longer serve us.

We replay conversations long after they have ended, convincing ourselves that if we analyze them enough, we can change their outcome. We resist change, thinking that if we surrender to uncertainty, we will lose control over our lives.

But letting go is not a weakness — although it's often mistaken for that. In truth, letting go is one of the greatest acts of strength. It's not about indifference, and it's not about walking away from challenges too soon. It's about recognizing when something costs you your peace, your voice, your self-respect – and choosing yourself anyway. It's understanding that not everything that once felt right is meant to stay and that letting something go doesn't erase its value. It simply means its purpose in your life has been fulfilled.

For so many years, I believed that strength meant holding on. I held on to people who had already let go of me, convincing myself that loyalty meant staying even when I wasn't valued anymore. I stayed in spaces that took everything out of me, believing that enduring them was proof of my resilience. I clung to ideas of who I thought I should be, shaping myself around expectations that were never truly mine.

But I've learned this the hard way — holding on to what hurts you, what depletes you, what no longer fits who you are becoming, that's not strength. Real strength is knowing when to walk away—not out of anger, but out of clarity and self-respect. And I've also learned that not everything is meant to be fought for.

There is a peace that comes when we finally release. When we stop resisting life, when we stop forcing people or situations to fit a story we've outgrown, we make space for healing, for joy, for the kind of freedom we were too afraid to allow before.

Letting go isn't about giving up. It's about giving yourself back. It's about trusting that what is truly meant for you will never require you to shrink or betray yourself to keep it.

We often think of letting go as a loss. But what if letting go is not the end of something but the beginning of everything? What if, by releasing what no longer serves us, we open space for something better, something we couldn't even imagine while holding on?

Imagine trying to fill a cup that's already overflowing — there's no room for anything new until we pour some of it out. The weight of what we refuse to release leaves no space for anything else to enter.

True presence isn't about erasing the past or pretending the future doesn't exist. It's about refusing to live from either one.

It's seeing the past as a teacher, not a chain. It's looking toward the future with openness, not fear, knowing that even though we can't predict what's coming, we can remain open enough to receive it.

And this is where presence and letting go meet – in that moment when we stop grasping and start trusting.

Because mastering presence is not a passive thing — it's a choice we make over and over again to return, to soften, to stay with what's real. And letting go isn't a one-time event. It's a practice. A lifelong journey of uncovering what's been hidden beneath all that we've carried.

Some things we will have to let go of more than once. Some wounds will reopen just when we thought they were healed. Some moments will ask us to surrender again and again. But with every release, we become lighter. With every surrender, we move closer to peace.

There is something so beautiful about trusting life, about believing that what has left was meant to leave, and what is on its way to us is already coming.

It's in that space — where we stop fighting, where we accept life as it is — that we find the kind of freedom that can't be taken away. It's opening your hands, your heart, and your life to everything that was always meant to find you.

THE SHIFT

The 24-Hour Life Test

Tomorrow morning, before the noise begins, before the world asks anything of you, give yourself one moment of stillness — and make a promise to yourself:

"For the next 24 hours, I will stop waiting to live my life."

Just a decision to stop postponing what matters. For one day, you will show up to your life as if it already belongs to you — not to the person you're trying to become, not to the healed version of you that hasn't arrived yet, but to you as you are right now.

- You'll speak the truth that's been sitting in your throat.
- You'll do the thing you've been delaying — maybe it's calling someone, starting something, wearing something you love, or simply allowing yourself to enjoy what you normally rush through.
- You'll move through your day without asking permission to feel joy or peace.

And when your mind starts whispering that it's not the right time, that you need to earn it first, that it should wait a little longer — meet that voice with care and remind it:

"I've spent enough of my life on pause."

This isn't about forcing anything. It's not about proving anything.

It's about choosing to stop holding your breath.

Living in the now doesn't mean everything is figured out. It means you no longer delay your life until it is.

So for 24 hours, let yourself be here fully — not halfway, not almost. Let yourself laugh without explanation, rest without guilt, and move without needing a reason. Create a moment you'll remember — not because it was extraordinary, but because you were in it.

And when the day is over, let it be enough. No need to reflect or analyze. Simply acknowledge that you showed up.

Say: **"Today, I lived. Not perfectly, but fully. And that is more than enough."**

Let this not be a one-time experiment but something you return to more often. A way of living that reminds you your life isn't waiting to begin. It's already happening — and you're allowed to live it now.

The past dissolved behind her, the future unfolded ahead,
but in the present, she chooses who she will become.

CHAPTER: 04

Becoming Who You Are – Reclaiming Your Mind & Building the Person You Want To Be

What Holds You Together: Discipline and Consistency

Discipline is not something you are born with, nor something that magically comes to you when you are inspired. It's what keeps you grounded when everything around you feels like it's falling apart. It's the invisible force of every single thing I have ever achieved and probably the only reason I'm still standing today.

I believe that discipline is often misunderstood. People think of it as some kind of superpower, but for me, discipline has never been a choice – it's been a necessity. It's been the one thing I could rely on when nothing else made sense.

When I was a child, I was like a little soldier, committed to my goals, structured in my thinking, and persistent in everything I set my mind to. I never needed anyone to remind me to do my homework or wake me up for school. I didn't need anyone to push me. I took that responsibility on myself because, deep down, I knew that if I didn't show up for myself, no one else would. I didn't grow up with privilege or comfort — I grew up in a reality that demanded resilience early. That kind of reality teaches you quickly that discipline isn't about being strong when things go easy but about staying committed when nothing feels certain.

I got my first dog when I was fourteen, and that little soul taught me more about discipline and responsibility than any human ever did. She wasn't just a pet — she was my entire world. I remember watching her sleep and feeling like nothing in the world mattered more than making sure she was safe, fed, loved, and never alone. I became more disciplined than I had ever been, waking up early to walk her, preparing her meals, caring for her when she was unwell, and putting her needs before my own — even when I was exhausted, even when I was hurting. I didn't miss a single day, not out of obligation, but because she trusted me with her life, and I took that seriously in a way most adults didn't expect from a teenager. That's when I understood: discipline isn't something you turn on and off when it's convenient — it's something that becomes part of you, especially when no one else understands why you're still showing up.

That same mindset followed me into adulthood. Whether it was pushing through the demanding years of medical school, staying diligent in my fitness routine despite tiredness, or showing up for work every day with complete dedication, I never relied on feelings to dictate my actions. Even in moments of physical pain or emotional hardship, I never let myself take the easy way out. There were countless days when I had every reason to slow down, make excuses, and justify doing less, but I never did. I have always believed that the moment you start negotiating with yourself, you start giving your power away.

And if there's one thing I've learned, it's this: discipline means doing the things, especially when you don't feel like it, and doing them anyway.

It's waking up at 5 am when you barely slept. It's pushing your body through a workout when you feel weak and your muscles ache. It's working on your dreams when everyone else is resting, nobody sees you, and no one will ever clap for you. It's saying no to the things that give you short-term comfort because you know they will steal your long-term peace.

But as much as I love discipline, I'm certain that discipline without consistency means nothing. Anyone can be discipline d for a week or a month when motivation is high and life feels exciting. However, consistency is what separates those who only talk from those who take action by staying committed month after month, year after year, decade after decade.

Consistency is showing up every single day, no matter how you feel, no matter how much you want to quit, no matter how small the progress seems. It's about steady, determined effort — even when motivation is gone, talent fades, and hope feels distant.

I've lost count of the days I wanted to give up — days when my body was drained, when my mind was overwhelmed, and I was fighting the silent battles that no one could see. Days when I asked myself: *"What's the point of trying so hard?"* But somewhere deep inside, I knew: If I stop, nothing will change. And if I don't save myself, no one will. So I kept going, not because I had all the power of this world, but because I refused to give up on the life I know I deserve.

People ask me all the time: *"How do you do it? How do you stay disciplined and consistent for years without stopping?"* And I tell them the truth: I don't give myself another option.

Because if you give yourself a way out — when you say, *"I'll do it tomorrow"* or *"I'll start again next week"* — you've already lost. Life doesn't pause when you're tired. Life doesn't wait for you to be ready. If you want something, you have to fight for it every single day, or you don't get it. That's the brutal truth nobody wants to say out loud.

And maybe that's why something my mother used to say became a principle I live by every day: "If you can do it today, don't leave it for tomorrow." Because nothing stays the same – the tea gets cold, we grow old, priorities change, and life moves on, whether you are ready or not.

I don't believe in that spark people call on to get started. It comes and goes — here one moment, gone the next. You can't build a life on something that drifts away when you need it most. I only believe in discipline and consistency, because they stay when everything else fades.

There will be failures. There will be moments of doubt. There will be moments when you feel that everything is falling apart. But discipline and consistency give you the power to stand up again, to keep going, and always have a way through.

No, I'm not perfect. And I'm not here to pretend I have it all figured out. I've had days when I've felt completely lost, days when I questioned if I had anything left to give. But somehow, I kept moving forward. And that's what discipline really is — not being strong, not perfect all the time – but simply refusing to give up.

So if you're sitting there wondering how to change your life, wondering why things never shift, let me tell you this:

Start showing up for yourself. Stop overthinking. Stop waiting for the right mood. Stop negotiating with yourself. You may never be ready, but you have to do it anyway.

Because in the end, life isn't shaped by what you do when things are easy. It's shaped by what you do when it feels impossible.

And one day, when you look back at everything you've accomplished — when people ask you how you did it — you'll know the truth.

It wasn't magic.

It wasn't luck.

It was you showing up again and again.

It was you staying in it, even when it hurt.

It was you refusing to give up, no matter how hard life can get.

And this is what will always separate those who live their dreams from those who only talk about them.

When Motivation Fails, Identity Leads

People don't fail because they lack potential. And it's not because we're not good enough. We fail because we let excuses run our lives. We wait, we delay, and we come up with perfectly crafted reasons that make us feel better about staying where it's safe, where it's familiar. But if we're really honest with ourselves, we know the only thing standing between us and the life we want is the story we keep repeating in our minds.

I've never allowed myself the luxury of excuses. Not even once. Even in the darkest moments of my life, I never let circumstances dictate my actions. I never let pain, desperation, or uncertainty become a justification for doing less.

But still, I hear people complaining every single day. Complaining about being overweight but refusing to step into a gym. Complaining about health but doing nothing to improve it. Complaining about toxic relationships but too afraid to walk away. Complaining about being broke, yet spending hours scrolling, watching, and wasting time instead of building something better. Complaining about being "too busy" — yet losing hours to social media, Netflix, mindless games, or empty conversations.

And then there's the one I hear the most: *"I don't have time."*

But let's be real — It's never about time – it's about what you decide to make a priority. You always make time for what truly matters.

And the most dangerous excuse of all? *"I will start on Monday."* The lie of "starting next week," "starting next month," and "waiting for the new year resolution" is nothing more than procrastination disguised as planning. We think we're "preparing" to do better, but what we're really doing is stalling. Every day you wait is a day you will never get back. And before you know it, months and years go by, and nothing has changed.

Procrastination is like a thief. It steals dreams while convincing you that you still have time. But time is passing — whether you do something about it or not. And every day, you have a chance to make a choice: to move closer to what you want, or to stay trapped behind your excuses.

The difference between those who succeed and those who stay stuck is not intelligence or talent — it's an action. Successful people do not wait for the right time because they know there is no right time. They do not wait to "feel ready" because they understand that readiness is just a deception. The only way forward is to start before you are ready. Start when it is uncomfortable. Start when it is inconvenient. Start when you do not feel like it. Because if you do not, you never will.

It's not about waiting for the right moment or the perfect mood — it's about deciding who you are and living from that place. You don't sit there debating with yourself about whether to show up — you show up because that's just what someone like you does. You act because you've already chosen to be the kind of person who does the hard things, no matter how you feel.

When motivation fails, identity takes over. The people who struggle with discipline are the ones who rely on motivation to push them forward, but motivation is unpredictable — it ebbs and flows, influenced by mood, energy , and circumstances. No one stays motivated forever. Those who seem unstoppable aren't driven by mood — they're driven by identity.

There is no weighing of options, no negotiation with themselves, no checking how they feel. The decision was made long before the moment came.

And here is what most people do not want to admit: No one is coming to save you. No one is going to force you to change your habits. No one is going to drag you out of bed and push you to take action. You're either committed, or you're not. You either get up and do the work, or you watch your life slip away, wasted on empty promises of "starting tomorrow."

The people who achieve their goals aren't the ones with more time, or more energy. They're the ones who stopped using how they feel as an excuse. They show up — especially when it's hard. That's what sets them apart.

At the end of the day, you can have results, or you can have excuses. But you cannot have both.

The Price of Mastery

Mastery doesn't come easily. It comes with a cost. Life eventually collects a toll from those who dare to want more than survival. It asks for the early mornings, the late nights, the choices that separate those who drift through life from those who transform it from within. Mastery requires sacrifice — not once, but constantly — until it's ingrained in how you live, think, and move through life. It is the process of burning away everything that is weak, everything that is comfortable, everything that keeps you away from the person you are meant to be.

People talk about success as something you stumble upon, as if it's handed to you by chance or accident. But mastery is an entirely different path — it has nothing to do with success. It doesn't come to those waiting for ideal circumstances. It doesn't belong to those who expect rewards without effort. It's earned by those willing to do what most avoid — those who understand that nothing worth having comes without a price.

I was never given an easy road. I had no family wealth, no inheritance, and no powerful last name to open doors for me. My parents refused to be members of any political party that might have made our lives easier. No one set the path before me or handed me opportunities. Everything I wanted, I had to fight for. Every step forward had to be earned, paid for in sacrifice, struggle, and the belief that I was capable of becoming someone greater than my circumstances.

At sixteen, while my peers spent their winter breaks in warmth and comfort, I was standing in the freezing cold at a petrol station, washing dirt-streaked car windows with hands cracked and raw from the biting wind. The air was so cold, my fingers numb, my body aching from hours of standing. But I was there for a reason — to make enough money to buy a bicycle, my only way to get to school, and I was not shy or humiliated to do what needed to be done.

There was no choice. I worked, or I went without. I paid the price with every battle I faced — every late night of studying, despite how drained I felt, every illness I fought through because I couldn't afford to stop, every moment I swallowed my pain and kept pushing forward — it all brought me here.

This wasn't a one-time hardship but a pattern that followed me for years. I took on seasonal jobs whenever I could find time away from my demanding studies, pushing myself through school, investing every spare bit of energy into my future — into English and French classes, learning, and building the person I wanted to become. While others around me were numbing themselves with alcohol, drugs, and clubs — trying to escape the emptiness that a decade of war had left behind — I was carrying my own burdens, knowing that every bit of effort I gave would lead me somewhere better.

And yet, while I fought for every step forward, I watched others take the easy way. I saw many women who had no desire to succeed, no desire to earn, no desire to create something of their own. They weren't interested in hard work, growth , or sacrificing for a greater future. They wanted instant gratification and the illusion of comfort — and they found both the easiest way they could: through men who could buy them the life they weren't willing to build themselves.

For these women, success had nothing to do with effort. Their ambition was measured by how much they could take from someone else. Their lives revolved around being desirable enough to be funded, kept, and taken care of. Their self-worth wasn't built on their own accomplishments but on how much a man was willing to give them in exchange for their subscription. They weren't interested in building themselves but in selling themselves. Attaching their futures to men who could offer them expensive vacations, luxury bags and clothes, prestigious cars to be driven in, and a comfortable life in return.

Everything seemed to revolve around money and sex — an endless game, as if there's nothing else in this life that matters. Nothing else to live for.

But that's not what real success is about.

A woman who builds nothing for herself owns nothing. A woman who trades her dignity for wealth is never truly rich. She becomes a product bought and sold. Her life is dependent on someone else's choices, at the mercy of someone else's desires. She may live in luxury, but she will never know the satisfaction of standing on her own, of looking at what she has and knowing it is hers. Not because she sold herself for it. But because she earned it.

And that was the one thing I swore — I would never be like them.

Because that thought still sickens me to my core.

I would rather rise through integrity than ever allow my life to be built on shortcuts and dependency. Because what I was building was mine, and it could never be taken away from me.

And that is what mastery is about — ownership.

It's about standing on your own two feet, knowing that everything you have is because of you. It's about self-respect. About knowing that you have earned your place — that your life is yours and no one else's. Mastery is about taking full responsibility for who you are and refusing to let anyone else dictate your worth.

The price of mastery is steep. It's choosing growth over comfort, enduring the frustration, the setbacks, and the long stretches where progress feels invisible. It's about trusting the process — even when the process feels like it's going nowhere.

But beyond the struggle and the ownership, mastery is also about freedom. Because when you build yourself, you own yourself. When you rely on no one to create the life you want, you walk through the world with certainty, knowing your success is yours, your choices are yours, and your life is not at the mercy of anyone else.

Mastery does not belong to a chosen few. It belongs to anyone willing to claim it — to those who refuse the easy path, who are willing to sacrifice for something greater than temporary pleasure. It belongs to those who endure the process, no matter how hard, because the only thing worse than the pain of becoming is the emptiness of never trying. Especially when all you're left with is a life that feels empty and fake.

This isn't just about victories or achievements. It's about the deep, unwavering knowledge that you are yours — and yours alone. And you are no one's to be claimed.

THE SHIFT

Integrity Week

This isn't about chasing motivation or waiting for the perfect mood. This is about living as the person you said you'd become. Not someday — but now, and not in theory — but in practice.

For the next seven days, you commit to one thing: showing up for yourself. Not to prove anything. But to build trust with the only person whose consistency truly matters — you.

Each morning, for one week, before the distractions of the day begin, choose three non-negotiables. Small daily promises. Just real actions that reflect the kind of life you're building. The kind of discipline that stays.

Here are some examples:

- Eat one nourishing, homemade meal
- Practice five minutes of stillness
- Finish something you've postponed
- Set a boundary — and keep it
- Go to sleep when you said you would

Put them in your calendar, set reminders, and make space for them. And then — do them. Not because it's easy. But because it's the kind of integrity you want to live by. Because it's the version of you that doesn't keep breaking your own word.

At the end of each day, ask yourself:

- "Did I follow through?"
- "Where did I show up?"
- "Where did I let myself off the hook?"

No writing, no journaling — just notice.

Because real change doesn't begin with motivation. It begins with noticing and then doing better.

By the end of the week, you won't be perfect — but you will have something rare and unshakable: evidence. Evidence that you can be counted on. That you keep your word. That you're becoming someone whose life is shaped by values, not moods.

That's how you become who you're meant to be.

One real decision at a time.

She kept climbing when no one was watching — that's how she became everything they said she couldn't be.

CHAPTER: 05

Turning Pain Into Power – How Struggles Shape Your Greatest Strengths

The Unseen Strength – What Pain Awakens

Unseen strength is not something we're born with. It's not something that appears when everything feels right, nor is it something you recognize when life is treating you kindly. It is something that is earned — something that emerges only when you are pushed beyond everything you thought you could endure. And when pain enters your life, when everything familiar is torn away, you're left with nothing but yourself, forced to face what you are truly made of.

In this society obsessed with shortcuts and artificial positivity, we're often told that a simple shift in mindset can solve our deepest struggles. *"Just think positive."* *"Be strong."* These phrases bother me every time I hear them because life isn't as simple as plastering a smile over open wounds. So, instead of trying to explain what I was going through, I began to dismiss it, saying: *"I'm perfectly fine,"* even when I wasn't.

For me, pain wasn't just an abstract idea or some magical aha moment waiting to be understood. It was my reality — something I lived with every single day. It shaped the way I thought, the way I moved, the way I saw myself, and the world around me. It wasn't asked for, it wasn't invited, but it became a force that carved itself into me in ways I never imagined I'd have to carry.

I've been through enough to know what it means to struggle — a difficult childhood, ongoing health battles, and years of personal and professional pressure. But nothing prepared me for what I faced after my most recent surgery — one of more than 20 I've had in my life. The pain wasn't just physical — it took over everything. Sitting, standing, and even walking became nearly impossible. Simple movements felt like a fight against my own body. There were moments I found myself on my knees, not from surrender, but because standing upright or lying down was no longer an option. I wasn't just recovering — I was forced to confront a version of myself I no longer recognized, stuck in a body that felt foreign and unresponsive.

But this wasn't the first time I had to fight through pain.

In 2016, I was in a car accident that wasn't my fault. My neck, lower back, and right hand were affected, and what followed was not just months but years of recovery, years of learning to live with injuries that never fully healed. Some remained, shaping the way I moved, the way I worked, the way I lived. I underwent multiple surgeries — first my wrist, then my shoulder — trying to reclaim what I had lost. But the hardest part wasn't just the physical pain; it was the realization that my entire profession, everything I had trained for, everything I had built, relied on a hand that would never be the same again.

Even when I couldn't work as I once did, I searched for new ways to move forward. I explored ideas outside my field, trying, failing, trying again. Not every attempt was a success, but I never felt ashamed of that because the only thing that would have made me feel like a failure was not trying at all.

After all these years, my right hand has never been like it used to be. There are still moments when pain shoots through it like an electric current, moments when it reminds me of everything I've been through. But it never stopped me. It never made me less. If anything, it made me fight harder, work smarter, and prove to myself more than anyone that I am so much more than what life tried to take from me.

When I felt most vulnerable, I realized that strength isn't about always having the answers or never breaking down. It's about being there for yourself, even when everything feels unbearably heavy. It's about acknowledging the depth of your pain and still choosing to move forward, not because you have to, but because there is a path to healing within that struggle. And that's what kept me going.

Writing a book has always been a passion of mine, but life always seemed to get in the way — studying, my career, the full-time responsibility of motherhood, taking care of my home, simply being too busy to make time for it. I kept postponing it, telling myself I'd start when I had more time.

But this time was now.

And as strange as it sounds, this pain became the perfect moment to finally write.

I never imagined writing a book this way. I pictured myself sitting comfortably at a desk, words flowing effortlessly, my thoughts clear and uninterrupted. Instead, I found myself in the complete opposite situation — writing in the midst of overwhelming pain.

My body refused to cooperate.

But my mind refused to surrender.

So, I wrote.

I wrote while lying down, shifting positions every few minutes just to keep the pain from swallowing me whole. I wasn't just writing words on a page — I was clawing my way through pain, sentence by sentence. It would have been so much easier to stop. To tell myself that healing had to come first, that I would write when things got better. But deep down, I knew something stronger than pain itself:

If I could write through this, I could write through anything.

So, it became my sanctuary.

It gave me a sense of peace and clarity that I had never experienced, not even in my entire career. For the first time, I felt truly alive. When everything felt like too much, writing became the one thing that still made sense. Through words, I processed my anguish, reflected on my experiences, and turned my suffering into something meaningful.

My experiences have taught me that pain , while unwelcome, can be a life-altering master. It has a way of showing us what nothing else can. It strips away everything superficial, revealing who we truly are and uncovering strengths we never knew we had. Seeing it this way doesn't take away the hardship, but it reminds us that even in our darkest moments, there's a chance to grow in ways we never expected.

By sharing my journey, I hope to offer something real to those facing their own struggles. It's not about ignoring pain or covering it up with empty positivity. It's about facing it with courage, allowing it to shape you, and coming out the other side with a deeper understanding of what you're truly capable of.

This is the unseen strength that pain awakens — a force that, once discovered, becomes an indelible part of who we are.

A strength born in darkness, but a strength that endures.

The Gift of Adaptation

I never thought I'd have to start over so many times. Not just to change my surroundings or begin a new job, but to start over in the deepest sense. In my body, in my identity, in the life I thought I was building.

Back in Serbia, my husband and I had a decent life. One we worked hard for. We weren't handed anything — we built it ourselves, brick by brick. A home, careers, and a sense of stability. But that safety was shattered twice when an armed gang broke into our house. They didn't just take what was ours; they could take away something we couldn't get back: our lives. Our stability and our feeling of being safe in our own home. After the second time, we knew we were no longer just living under threat — we were living with a target on our backs. And the saddest part? In Serbia, this kind of violence had become normal — just another part of daily life in a country where peace always feels out of reach, corruption runs deep, and deep down, I had come to believe that things would never truly get better.

It was a life full of pressure in every way — no safety, no security, you could lose your life in a second. A country that lives under the control of its own mafia. They wanted us to give ourselves to something we didn't believe in — to join a political party that we had no faith in, that didn't align with who we were. And when we refused, the message became clear: stay and surrender who you are, or leave and risk everything to begin again. I never wanted my children to live in those awful conditions or to ever experience the kind of childhood and life I once had.

So, we chose to leave. We packed up our lives, not because we were chasing something bigger, but because we were protecting something sacred — our integrity, our values, our family. We carried our whole lives in suitcases and walked away from everything that once felt like home. We landed in a place where even the air felt different, where nothing and no one felt familiar — and yet, we chose to stay. We chose to begin again, with empty hands but an unbreakable spirit, building a new life from the kind of strength most people never had to find. We came to Dubai with a two-year-old in our arms and another baby on the way. We didn't know what was waiting for us. The only way out was through, and we knew we had to take that first step.

The beginning was tough, so much heavier than anyone could see from the outside. We were promised a future that disappeared the moment we arrived. The people who had brought us here for work turned their backs. We had no health insurance, no support system, and not even enough money to fill our fridge. Even though my husband worked so hard to make ends meet, we still struggled. Everything was unfamiliar — the language, the culture, the rules, the way people moved through life. I had no friends, no one to call if something went wrong, no one to sit with and say: *"This is hard, and I'm scared."*

As if that wasn't enough, shortly after we arrived in Dubai, I received the news that my father had been diagnosed with an incurable form of cancer — and was given only a few years to live. And it broke me completely. Still, I had to keep going. I had little ones who needed me, who didn't know how much I was holding inside, only that I showed up. So I did. Every day, even when I felt tired, unsure, and anxious about what might come next. I kept going — not because I felt ready, but because I knew staying stuck wasn't an option. Something in me refused to stop there.

There was one thing I was certain of: I would never return to that corrupted country again.

Dubai became my only home, the only place where my heart and soul truly belong. Even though it was hard and uncertain, this city gave me a new life.

That's what adaptation really is. Not the polished version we post online or look back on years later as if it were simple. It's raw, messy, and sometimes overwhelming. It's waking up in a foreign country with no one to turn to, yet still finding a way to keep going. It's choosing not to quit, even when the world around you feels like it's closing in.

I changed because I had to survive. I had to let go of everything I thought I knew about how life was supposed to look, about who I was supposed to be. There wasn't space for the old version of me anymore. She wouldn't have made it through those days.

I wore so many roles I could barely keep track — mother, wife, provider, immigrant, doctor, woman trying to hold it all together. Some days, I felt like I was doing it all. On other days, I was barely holding on. But through it all, I was slowly learning to move differently, to listen more deeply, and to stop trying to force life into the shape I once thought it needed to be.

And somewhere along the way, I softened. Not in weakness — but in wisdom. I stopped needing everything to make sense. I stopped gripping so tightly to my plans. I allowed life to show me new ways to be strong — ways that didn't require me to fight but to trust.

Adaptation isn't about pretending you're fine. It's about being honest with where you are — and still finding a way to move forward with intention. It's about letting life stretch you without snapping. It's about meeting the hardest moments with an open heart — not because you're fearless, but because you believe there's still something good waiting on the other side.

And there was. Not all at once, but slowly, day by day, I began to rebuild. Not the life I thought I was supposed to live, but the life that was meant for me now. One rooted in presence, resilience, and grace.

I look back now and realize the weight of those difficult times didn't break me. It revealed me. It didn't just change me – it brought me back to the person I was always meant to be. And maybe that's the gift. Not that things turned out perfectly. But I found my way through, anyway.

The Graceful Rise

I didn't notice I was changing at first. There was no single moment where everything clicked into place, no clear sign to announce the beginning of something new. The shift was slow and almost invisible, unnoticeable to anyone but me. It came in how I responded to the same chaos with less urgency. It came in choosing not to explain myself, even when silence felt uncomfortable. It came in deciding to walk away — not to punish, not to prove a point, but simply to protect my peace. It came in lying down to rest while my mind still clung to the belief that I hadn't done enough to deserve it. This time, something felt different.

And yet, that's where everything began.

This wasn't the kind of growth that starts with hope. It began with depletion. In the heaviness of a body that had been running for too long. I had been in survival mode for years, moving from one crisis to another, constantly fixing, managing, and holding together what kept falling apart. I had become so used to functioning under pressure that I forgot what it felt like to exist without the weight. And because I was still standing, I thought that meant I was fine. But surviving is not the same as living, and I was just beginning to understand that difference.

What changed wasn't my circumstances. Life didn't suddenly soften for me. The responsibilities were still there. The uncertainty, the noise, the expectations — they didn't disappear. What changed was the way I met them. I stopped waiting for life to calm down so I could feel peace, and instead started creating peace within myself, even in the midst of it all. I stopped chasing control and started choosing presence . I began to ask myself what actually felt right instead of what looked right. I no longer wanted to perform resilience — I wanted to embody it, to live it from a place that didn't leave me empty.

I started noticing the woman I was becoming, not the one I had tried so hard to prove myself to be. She didn't speak as loudly. She didn't try to impress anyone. She didn't need to explain her worth. She had walked through fire and was no longer afraid of burning. And that strength didn't come from achievement or grit. It came from self-respect. From boundaries. From the decision to stop betraying herself for the sake of being understood.

The transformation was sacred. I began living with myself, not against myself. I learned to stay. Not just physically, but emotionally. I stayed when it was uncomfortable. I stayed when I wanted to be numb, escape, or pretend. I stayed with the ache, with the grief, with the parts of me I used to push away. And in doing so, I finally heard what my body had been trying to say all along: *We're tired. We want to be held. We want to feel safe inside ourselves again.*

I began listening.

I stopped rushing through the day just to check things off a list. I began moving slower, but more intentionally. I stopped criticizing my reflection and started offering it compassion. I nourished my body with care, not punishment. I moved not to shrink, but to feel more alive inside my skin. I stopped chasing the illusion of some future version of me that would finally be enough and started acknowledging that everything I am today is already worthy of tenderness, grace, and rest.

This wasn't the kind of rise that others could witness from the outside. There was no reinvention, no arrival, and no applause. But something in me had shifted so profoundly that I knew I would never go back to the way things were. Because I no longer wanted to live in survival. I wanted to live in truth. In alignment. In peace that didn't require perfection to exist.

It came the moment I forgave myself for the years I spent abandoning my own needs just to hold everything together. It came when I stopped waiting for someone to choose me and finally chose myself instead. It came when I finally understood that I didn't need to go back to who I was — I had outgrown that version. I was becoming someone far more whole.

This is what it means to grow beyond survival.

To live without apology.

To feel safe in your own presence.

To build a life that doesn't drain you just to maintain it.

To look around and realize you're no longer holding your breath — you're breathing fully. Like you were always meant to.

This is the rise I never expected.

Not louder. Not brighter.

Just truer.

And entirely mine.

THE SHIFT

The Endurance Practice

Pain changes you – but what you choose to do with it is where endurance is built. That's where the real work begins.

This shift isn't about letting go. It's about creating something that stays — a moment in your day, not to escape discomfort but to meet it fully. A daily reminder that you already have what it takes to keep going, even when life gets hard again.

Here's the practice:

Choose one physical action that challenges you. Something small but difficult.

Something that requires effort, discomfort, and presence.

Examples:

- Holding a plank for 60 seconds
- Walking up and down stairs 5 times without stopping
- Finishing every shower with 30 seconds of cold water, breathing through it
- Sit on the floor and stand up — without using your hands. Do it 5 times
- Running or walking a fixed distance every day

Whatever you choose, do it daily — for 21 days.

Not to test your limits.

Not to chase results.

But to train your body and mind to stay — when it aches, when it resists, when you want to quit.

Every time you show up, you remind your nervous system: "I can **meet discomfort with power. I've done it before. I'm doing it again."**

There's no comparison.

No outcome to perform for.

Just truth, effort, and presence — one honest moment at a time.

You're not healing to become someone new.

You're building the resilience to live as who you already are.

She didn't rise from the fire. She grew from the ashes.

CHAPTER: 06

Finding Your Worth – Breaking Free In A World That Profits Off Your Insecurities

The Illusion of Image

Social media is a powerful tool — if we know how to use it. It can educate, inspire, uplift, and connect us in meaningful ways. I find genuine joy in supporting animal shelters, donating to charities, helping children in need, and sharing causes that deserve attention. I love watching heartwarming animal rescue videos that restore my hope in humanity, discovering gluten-free and plant-based recipes, getting inspired by new yoga flows, and learning from people who share wisdom with humility and depth. I also enjoy seeing beautiful travel scenery — places I've never been, cultures I've yet to explore, and corners of this incredible world that remind me how much beauty still exists. That, to me, is the kind of content that adds actual value to each day.

But more often than not, that's not what we see.

Instead of being a space for learning, compassion, and awareness, it's become a place filled with comparison , jealousy, and judgment. People scroll for hours, not realizing how much it takes away their peace. A single photo of someone's life is enough to trigger feelings of unworthiness — to question your own path or to assume someone else has it better. And what's worse is that much of what's posted isn't even real.

We live in a time where showing off has replaced living. Where people pause real moments just to post them, as if something only matters when others see it. What I find sad isn't just how often it happens but how normal it's become. Everyone wants to be seen, noticed, and praised. As if worth must be proven through likes and comments. People chase attention for the most ordinary parts of life.

Branded bags, designer shoes, manicured hands gripping the wheel of a luxury car. Diamond rings, soft smiles, private jet fantasies — all starting to look the same. It's less about sharing life and more about proving something, though no one ever says exactly what. And we're somehow expected to be impressed by someone filming themselves lifting weights at the gym. But honestly, why does that matter? Since when did we start confusing our self-worth with gym reps and mirror selfies? Or when someone proudly says: "French made" or "American born" — what does that even mean in the story of your character? What difference does it make where your passport was printed if your presence carries no depth?

The same poses, the same locations, the same captions — just slightly rearranged. It's all become about how much you have, how perfect you look, and how much attention you can get for it. And in the pursuit of that attention, many begin to lose touch with themselves completely.

I've never needed to prove anything online. Yes, I have the bags, the shoes, the lifestyle. And I can afford it. But when I buy something for myself, it's because I genuinely love it, not because of the brand name or the attention it might bring. If I wear something beautiful, it's for me. I don't need a logo to validate my value. And I certainly don't need strangers to confirm that I'm living well to feel secure in my life.

Because it's not just about material things anymore. Some have gone even further, reducing themselves to their body parts. Exposing their naked bodies, bending over backwards — literally — for likes, views, and gifts from strangers. It's disheartening to witness how many believe they must sell their image to feel seen or valuable. That somehow, attention equals worth — but it doesn't.

The best moments of my life? They never made it to social media. The real, raw, meaningful moments — those that changed, humbled, and made me who I am — weren't for show. They were for living. And the hardest ones? The ones that broke me open? I kept those private, too. Because let's be honest — not everyone needs access to your joy or pain. Someone once said, *"Twenty percent don't care about your problems — and eighty percent are glad you have them."* And it stayed with me. Not everything is meant to be shared, and not everyone watching is wishing you well.

I keep what's precious to me far from the public eye — my children, my family, my car, and my home. I protect them, not because I'm hiding, but because not everything sacred needs to be shared. Not everything valuable belongs on display. Some things are better when they're just yours, safe, grounded, untouched by judgment, comparison, and, most importantly, the evil eye.

I train my body daily, but you won't find me posting about every workout. I move because I respect my health and care for the body that's carried me through everything. I don't need a gym mirror or flexed pose to remind me I'm strong — I feel it in how I live, not how I look.

Even the food I prepare — when I share a photo, it's because there's something in it for someone else. A recipe, a tip, something nourishing. Not just a pretty plate for attention. I cook because I love to, because it brings joy and comfort. Because food should be about connection, not competition.

And then there are the questions people ask that feel like a complete intrusion — *Where are you from? Are you married? How old are you?* I don't understand how we've accepted these as normal conversation starters. Where I come from, those are considered deeply impolite. They reduce a person to labels and make everything about age, status, and social categories.

It's all become a game of social chess — who follows whom, who comments where, who supports whose content. And it's rarely genuine. I've seen people unfollow someone simply because they didn't get a "like back." As if connection should come with conditions. It is as if we've forgotten what it means to be real with one another. I remember reading the phrase: *"Like for like, follow for follow."* It's all so transactional – it's all so empty. And underneath it, you can sense it — a constant desperation to feel important.

It's strange to witness how far we've strayed from depth. People could choose to express something meaningful, something honest. But instead, many follow the crowd, posting what they think will be liked, even when it says nothing about who they really are. And maybe that's the heart of it: so many are chasing approval, forgetting that being yourself doesn't require permission.

Most of what you see on social media is only a fragment of the truth. That tiny little screen doesn't know what you carry. And it will never measure what matters. Because the most valuable parts of yourself are not visible.

And the image they see will never matter more than the truth you live.

Why Be a Copy When You Were Born an Original

There's never been more freedom to express who we are, but somehow, fewer people are actually doing it. With endless tools to create, connect, and stand out, it's almost unsettling how quickly so many give up on originality in exchange for what looks acceptable.

You'd think freedom would spark truth — but instead, so many still hold back. They imitate celebrities, hide behind filters, and shape themselves to match whatever's trending. Because somewhere along the way, blending in started to feel safer than being seen.

And I get it.

We were raised in a culture that profits from insecurity, so we follow what feels safer — dressing like her, speaking like her, contouring our faces until we barely recognize them, just to feel like we might finally belong.

But belong where?

To a life that looks good in pictures but doesn't feel like yours when you're living it?

I see it all the time at work. Women walk into my clinic —young, old, from every background — many of them already beautiful in ways they can't even see, and they show me photos of someone else.

"I want cheeks like this."

"Can you lift my brows to look like hers?"

"I want my face to look exactly like this filter."

And far too often, it's followed by:

"My husband prefers fuller lips."

"My boyfriend likes bigger curves."

I've heard it all.

And the question beneath it isn't really about beauty — it's about being enough, being love d, being accepted. But when your sense of worth depends on reshaping yourself to match someone else's vision, you're not being embraced — you're being tolerated for a version of yourself you created to avoid rejection.

What stays with me is how often they want to remove the things that make them unforgettable — features shaped by their genetics, personality, and energy. The things that make them real. Instead, they ask for what's trending, what's familiar, what feels easier to digest in a world of sameness. And most of the time, it's not even for themselves — it's to please someone else, to be approved, to avoid being left behind.

And I understand the pressure. Social media has taken comparison to a whole new level. We see these "influencers" whose entire presence revolves around being seen, but I've never understood it. I've never quite grasped the idea of being a blogger or influencer when there's no message, meaning, or contribution — just carefully arranged outfits, filtered smiles, and paid collaborations disguised as inspiration. What exactly are they influencing? What are they building? What are they offering, other than a life designed to be approved by others?

We've glamorized imitation and forgotten the beauty of individuality. We've made people believe that being followed is more valuable than being known. And the damage that does to our sense of self, especially for young people still trying to figure out who they are, is something we'll be unpacking for generations.

As for me, I've never felt drawn to that path. Not because I haven't felt the pressure — I have. But my life was shaped by something else entirely. I wasn't surrounded by constant praise. I never learned to seek attention or feel comfortable living in the spotlight. I grew up in an environment that required presence , clarity, and staying close to what's real. It was simply the truth. And the truth has always mattered more to me than fitting into a box that was never mine to begin with.

I never had the desire to adjust myself just to fit into someone else's idea of "enough." That didn't come from arrogance. It came from self-respect. From knowing I'd rather be misunderstood for being myself than accepted for being a version of someone else.

Choosing not to become what the world expects doesn't require a statement. It means staying close to yourself even when no one is cheering. It means making decisions that come from within, not from pressure. It means honoring your own voice — even when it's not echoed back at you.

That's not always easy.

There will be days you feel invisible. Times when staying true to yourself goes unnoticed, while noise and surface-level appeal get all the attention. But here's what I know: when you keep ignoring your own voice to meet the world's expectations , something sacred within you starts to fade. You slowly lose the connection to what feels real. Bit by bit, you stop recognizing what you actually want, what you care about, what makes you feel alive. And whatever you gained along the way won't be worth what you had to give up to get there.

You don't need to adjust to be chosen.

You don't need to soften or shrink to be accepted.

And if someone can't recognize what's real in you, they were never meant to hold that space in your life.

You were born an original. And that alone is your power.

Not because it demands attention, but because it holds truth.

And what's real will always outlast everything else.

You Don't Need to Be Fixed — You Need to Be Heard

I was always hesitant about joining social media. Not because I didn't have something to share, but because I wasn't sure where I belonged in a space that often felt more like a stage than a reality. I was already living a full life — raising my two children, caring for my home and my pets, working, studying, showing up for the people I love, and managing all the moving pieces that come with that. I wasn't pausing to publish those moments — not because they weren't meaningful, but because I was in them. I never felt the urge to ask for approval for something that already felt real to me.

But over time, that changed. At almost every professional meeting or event — even with my patients — I kept hearing the same question:

"What's your Instagram page?"

And when I said I didn't have one, the reactions were always the same — confused, amused, and slightly worried. It was like saying I'd missed the last decade. As if being offline made me outdated, old school, and invisible. It didn't matter what I was doing in real life — if it wasn't online, it didn't seem to count.

Eventually, I realized that social media had become a kind of social proof and a new form of credibility. If you weren't visible there, you weren't relevant. And while I didn't agree with it, I understood it. I knew that if I wanted to be seen in my field — truly seen — I needed to find a way to be present in that world without losing myself to it.

So, I created a space.

Not to impress or compete — but to reflect who I am and what I care about. A place where I could speak about skincare and health, share glimpses of travel and food, honor my love for animals, wellness, movement, and the beauty I find in simplicity. It wasn't about becoming someone new but giving my existing life a place to be seen.

But even with that clarity, social media has never been easy to navigate. It often feels like a place where everyone's selling something or themselves. Where true connection gets lost beneath the polished surface. Where the pressure to keep up can pull even the most grounded person off balance. It's not because the platforms are harmful — it's because they're designed to reward visibility over authenticity. And before you even notice it, you're twisting, compromising, and reshaping yourself just to feel like you belong.

There were times I caught myself drifting. Posting out of pressure instead of intention. Wondering if I should share more, do more, show more — not because I wanted to, but because I felt I had to. And that's when I would stop, pull back, and return to myself.

Because the real strength isn't in the content — it's in the self-respect to know your limits. The strength is knowing when to step away before you start living a version of yourself that isn't yours.

I've taken social media breaks and detoxes, often without announcing them. Quietly disappearing from the noise so I could reconnect with the parts of me that don't need to be validated. And every time, I was reminded: nothing I've ever posted has brought me as much peace as the moments I've lived off-screen.

You don't have to be louder to be heard.

You don't have to be everywhere to be meaningful.

And you don't have to trade your presence for popularity.

Take your time. Take your space. Take your energy back.

And let it be enough to live fully, whether anyone is watching or not
.
You were never too much. You were just unheard in too many places that never knew how to hold you.

You don't need to be fixed — you just need space to be fully known exactly as you are.

THE SHIFT

The Private Life Practice

Choose one part of your life and make it completely private — not as an act of hiding but as an act of self-respect.

Something you've been unconsciously offering to the world, shaping and reshaping to be seen, posted, shared, and validated. Something sacred like:

- Your relationship
- Your children
- Your healing
- Your joy
- Your daily routine
- Your future plans
- Or even the way your body is changing

Whatever you choose, let it stay fully yours. Not to be concealed, but to be lived without adjusting it for anyone else. You don't need to dress it up, explain it, or leave hints for others to notice. You simply stop sharing it.

The moment you stop molding it around what others might see or think, it begins to become something real. At first, you may feel the discomfort of being unseen. The reflex to stay active in spaces where attention once made you feel valuable. But if you sit with it, that noise fades. And in its place, you start to hear your own rhythm again — the sense of self that isn't tied to being looked at or liked.

You begin to remember that not everything meaningful needs to be seen.

Some things lose their meaning the moment you try to explain them. Joy doesn't ask to be noticed. And pain doesn't become more real just because it's shared.

This practice isn't about logging off or deleting anything. It's about staying exactly where you are without continuing to give your life away in pieces. It's about moving through your day without bending your choices around what might get attention. It's about keeping one part of your world untouched — not managed, not adapted, not reduced.

You're not hiding — you're choosing what stays yours.

And slowly, you realize this was never a detox — it was a return. A moment where you stopped handing yourself over and started living like your life belongs to you again.

That is the shift.

Not from social media — but from the habit of needing to be seen in order to exist.

What makes you real will never be measured in numbers.

CHAPTER: 07

The Connections You Keep – Cultivating Mindful & Meaningful Relationships

Don't Call Me When It's Convenient

You know that text.

The one that starts with, "Hey, how are you?" A couple of polite, sweet words that feel more like bait than care. Because it never stops there. It always leads to a favor, a request, an expectation that you'll fix whatever there is.

I never used to think twice. I was always the one to show up. Always the one to extend a hand, offer my time, my money, my energy, without hesitation. It wasn't kindness for the sake of recognition or acknowledgment. It was just me. It was my nature to give.

I paid bills when they were on the verge of being cut off, not because I had excess, but because I couldn't bear the thought of someone I cared about struggling. When they needed a place to stay, I made room. Even when my own circumstances were tight, I opened my home and gave them what little comfort I could offer. Not because I wanted anything back. But because I believed friendship meant showing up when it was hardest. I listened and wiped the tears when people were going through divorce, heartbreak, even while my own problems were demanding attention.

When I first arrived in the United Arab Emirates, I was learning how to build my life from scratch. I had nothing but determination and the will to make something out of the unknown. And yet, even as I was finding my own light, I found myself fighting for others. I sent CVs, reached out to contacts, made calls, wrote recommendation letters, and pushed opportunities their way. Even when I was in no position to help myself, and never once asking for favors for my own sake, I helped when I had no help. I gave when I had nothing to gain.

Because I used to care. Deeply.

They say if you want to lose a friend, lend them money. I understand that now. I've lost more than I can count. So many owe me — not just financially, but emotionally. And when, for the first time in my life, I needed something for myself — when I was drowning in medical bills, when my health insurance gave up on me, after years and years of battling for my health, when I simply asked for my money back — what I got in return was shouting, excuses and disrespect.

Suddenly, my years of helping, supporting, listening — it all evaporated the moment I asked for something that was rightfully mine. Where were they when I was struggling to hold myself together? When was I unable to stand or walk or even exist without pain? Because for the first time, I was the one who needed help.

They were gone. Not a single call to check on me. Not a single message asking how I was managing. The real shock was understanding it wasn't just strangers or distant acquaintances who treated me this way. It was the people I considered closest to me. The ones who had called me their friend, their sister, their family. The ones who enjoyed eating my food, sleeping in my bedsheets, wearing my clothes, using my home like a hotel, all while hiding behind words they never meant.

How many times did people come to me for free treatments, pretending it was about friendship, when really it was about access? How many times did they exploit my profession, my dedication, without ever thinking about the years of work, the sleepless nights, the sacrifices I had made to be where I am? They took my expertise for granted. They believed they were entitled to what I had built.

I never asked for anything in return. I believed that if you give from the heart, it should never feel like a transaction, and it should be considered the highest form of generosity. Not even a genuine "thank you." But what I never realized was that while I was giving with open hands, they were taking with greed and expectation.

But I realize now, there's a difference between giving from the heart and allowing yourself to be exploited. There's a difference between kindness and sacrificing your own well-being.

And that difference is called self-respect.

This is where I draw the line, not out of resentment but out of a deep understanding of what I deserve. I will not allow people to use me as their lifeline only when it is convenient for them. My time has value.

My energy has limits.

My kindness is no longer available for those who treat it like currency to be spent and used.

I have spent too much of my life trying to be everything for everyone. Giving and giving until there was nothing left for me.

The line has been drawn.

And it's a line I will never erase.

The Ones Who Stayed

Somewhere along the way, I stopped giving myself to those who never intended to stay. I stopped measuring my worth by how much

I could give to people who only valued what was easy. It took time to understand that not everyone deserves access to your heart. Life teaches you, sometimes painfully, that not everyone is meant to remain.

People come and go, but their leaving doesn't diminish your value — it reveals it. It sharpens your clarity, defines your boundaries, and separates what was real from what was never truly yours. It shows you who was meant to stay, not through promises or empty words, but through the steady strength of their presence when everything else falls away.

But the beauty of loss is that it reveals the truth of what remains and what endures. And what refuses to leave.

The ones who stay are the ones who define everything that holds true value. They are the ones who hold your hand when the world feels unforgiving, who carry your pain as if it is their own. They are the ones who prove that love is not something you chase, convince, or plead for. It is something you build, something you earn, something you cherish with everything you have.

People who belong in your life are those who hold space for you when your own strength fades. They don't demand explanations or offer judgment. They stay through the darkness, through the beauty, through the ordinary days that often matter most.

For me, everything begins and ends with my family.

My sons, are the most profound proof of what it means to be loved beyond condition, beyond expectation. From the moment I held them, I understood that real love is not something that demands. It gives, it protects, and it grows. Being their mother is more than a responsibility; it is a privilege that fills me with gratitude every single day. I promised them a life far better than the childhood I once had. A life built on acceptance and love. A life where their dreams are not dismissed but encouraged. A life where they know they are seen and valued exactly as they are. And every day, I honor that promise with everything I have. They are my greatest truth, my deepest purpose, and my most valuable gift.

And beside me is the man who has walked with me through everything. My husband, whose loyalty does not require explanation, whose kindness does not need justification. Our bond is not defined by perfection. It is defined by the decision to keep moving forward, together, even when the path is unclear. He has been my anchor and my strength, my resilience and my calm. What we share is something built through presence and perseverance, through acceptance and understanding. It is a love that remains even when life becomes harsh. It is a love that chooses to stay.

He has held my hand when there were no words. He's seen me at my most fragile and never once made me feel weak. We've grown not just beside each other but also because of each other — evolving through every season life has given us. And while the world may never see all that we've faced, I carry the certainty that with him, I am safe, I am seen, and I am home.

The pets I have welcomed into my life have given me a love that feels pure and uncomplicated. They have taught me that loyalty is not something spoken or promised — it is something given freely, without hesitation. They are as much a part of my family as anyone with a voice. Their presence fills my life with a joy that can never be replaced. In their simplicity, they have taught me more about devotion than most people ever could. They exist without an agenda. Their love is not transactional. It is given freely, and it is received with the same honesty. It is the comfort of knowing that real love just simply exists in its purest form.

True friendships are not something you find. It's something you build. It's something you recognize in those who stay. The ones who show up without being asked, who offer kindness when it would be easier to walk away. The ones who don't measure their affection by how much they receive but by how deeply they care. They are the ones who understand that friendship is not about perfection or agreement. It is about accepting you fully and encouraging you to grow into who you were always meant to be.

I have seen the difference between those who pretend to care and those who genuinely do. And I have let go of everyone who only saw me as a convenience, a benefit, a temporary source of comfort. Because what remains is far more valuable than what was lost.

The friends who have stayed are not many. But they are real. They are the ones who have proven their place in my life, not through words but through actions. And it is a gift – the one I will never take for granted.

This chapter is not about loss. It is about understanding the beauty of those who stay. It is about valuing the connections that endure, the love that remains when everything else falls away. It is about those who continue to choose you, not because of what you can offer, but because of who you are. It is about those who see you clearly, even when you struggle to see yourself.

To the ones who stayed, you are my proof that love is real. You are the reason I continue to create, to grow, to build something worthy of the devotion you have shown me. You are the reason I refuse to settle for anything less than what is genuine.

People will cross your path, but only those who truly belong in your life matter. And it is for them that I give everything I have. It is for them that I continue to build a life that will stand through every test, every challenge, every moment of doubt.

The ones who stay are not simply part of my life. They are the reason I believe in it. And that will always be enough.

Real Without Apology

I've always believed that to live truthfully means honoring your inner voice — what brings you joy, fulfillment, and peace. But many people never get to do that — not because they don't hear their truth, but because they've spent years being taught to ignore it.

They stay in marriages that drain their spirit to meet cultural expectations. They pursue careers that leave them numb to satisfy family pressure or financial needs. They hide parts of themselves just to be accepted.

These aren't rare stories — they're the kind of lives people are expected to accept without ever asking if they want them. A woman who never got to choose love. A man clocking into a job that erodes his spirit. A person slowly reshaping who they are to avoid rejection.

These aren't small choices — they're what slowly pull people away from who they really are. And while following the rules may look easier on the surface, the cost is your vitality, your voice, your truth.

Here's what I've come to understand: living authentically isn't about trying to meet anyone else's expectations. It's about alignment. It's about the relief and clarity that comes from choosing yourself unapologetically. From living a life where your thoughts, words, and actions all reflect who you truly are.

I choose to live this way because anything else would be a betrayal of my soul. It's not about fighting against the world or proving anyone wrong. It's about living in a way that feels genuine and fulfilling. And when you do that, you attract the right people, the right experiences, and the right kind of joy.

Living authentically isn't about perfection. It's about feeling at peace with yourself. It's the relief of knowing you no longer have to edit yourself to fit into someone else's idea of who you should be. It's making decisions that feel right to you, even when they don't make sense to anyone else. So, I decided to stop asking for permission to be myself. To live without apology.

Choosing authenticity has brought me clarity, peace, and connections that feel meaningful. It's shown me that the right people will always find their way to you when you are true to yourself. And the ones who fall away were never meant to stay.

This isn't about rejecting the world. It's about embracing yourself. It's about trusting that your desires, your dreams, your truth are enough. That your worth doesn't depend on anyone's approval but your own.

It's not about turning your back on the world — it's about choosing to no longer disappear inside it. It's about recognizing that your truth, your pace, your way of living — even if it doesn't make sense to anyone else — is still yours to honor. And when you stop molding your life around other people's comfort, something shifts. You move differently. You carry yourself with conviction. And for the first time, your life feels like it fits — not because it's flawless, but because it's finally yours.

Being real won't always be easy — but it will always be worth it.

Because nothing feels more like freedom than finally becoming someone you recognize.

THE SHIFT

The Access List

People treat you based on the access you allow.

And for most of your life, you gave full access — no passwords, no limits. Because you thought being available meant being kind. But now, you know better: love without boundaries is how you lose yourself.

This shift isn't about deleting people.

It's about building a system that honors your worth and energy.

Here's the shift:

On your phone — not on paper, not in theory — open your notes and divide a list into three sections:

- **Inner Circle** (Those who show up, who listen, who give back)
- **Limited Access** (Those who are inconsistent, one-sided, or draining)
- **No Longer Needed** (Those who only come around when it benefits them)

Inner Circle

These are the people who have stood beside you without needing attention or reminders. They've been steady in the chaos. Present when it counted. They've seen your strength and your mess and never used either against you. Honor them. Nourish these connections. Make space for them the way they've always made space for you. Because they're not just part of your life — they're part of your becoming.

→ Let them know. Reach out. Make time. Keep them close.

Limited Access

These are the people who sometimes care but rarely carry. You've waited long enough for them to show up the way you've shown up for them. It's not anger you feel — it's clarity. You've simply reached the point where your energy no longer flows where it isn't received. You don't need to explain the distance. You just stop overextending for those who've stayed comfortable on the edge of your life.

→ Loosen the connection. Respond less. Protect your energy without guilt.

No Longer Needed

There are some people who taught you through absence. People who once stood close but vanished the moment you needed them to show up. And even when they reappeared, it was never about you — it was about what you could give. But now, you're choosing something different.

Not bitterness. Not blame. You're choosing to release the weight of people who never knew how to carry you.

→ Don't explain. Just detach. Archive, mute, unfollow — and move forward.

This shift is not about changing others.

It's about finally respecting the one who kept showing up through it all: you.

This is how you protect your life without building walls.

This is how you honor your heart without closing it.

You don't need the world behind you – just the ones who never left.

CHAPTER: 08

Reclaiming Your Energy – Strengthening Your Mind, Body & Soul

Freeing Yourself from Punishment

Growing up during the war, food was never a certainty, and it wasn't something we talked about. It wasn't a joy or a choice, just a basic need that often wasn't met. Meals were small, irregular, and rarely enough. It taught me early on that wanting more was pointless, so my body grew thin and brittle. There was never enough, and I stopped questioning it. When life offers so little, you learn to accept less. You learn to convince yourself that less is all you deserve.

That scarcity stayed with me, even after the circumstances changed. My body had grown around the idea of "just enough," and so had my mind. Thinness felt familiar. So when my body began to change with puberty, I didn't welcome it. I didn't understand it. The softness, the weight, the curves — they felt uncomfortable, almost wrong. Not because they were, but because I had learned that control meant shrinking, and shrinking meant safety.

I gained weight, as every child does. But the world around me turned that natural growth into something shameful. My classmates tore me apart with their words, calling me fat with such conviction that I began to believe them. I had already been an outsider, bullied for being the nerd who cared about school more than anything. Now, I was the fat nerd, an easy target for cruelty from every direction. Their words followed me everywhere, instilled deep within me, long after the school day ended.

But the harshness didn't stop at school. Home was just another place for judgement. I remember my uncle visiting, always armed with jokes that were meant to be harmless but felt like stings. He would point at my stomach and laugh, calling it sausages and layers of fat, and everyone else would laugh along. I was only twelve, maybe thirteen, but the damage was already done. His words buried themselves deep within me, leaving scars no one could see.

It's a special kind of pain when the people who are supposed to protect you are the ones who wound you the most. I was too young to understand those "jokes". All I understood was that my body was wrong. That my existence needed correction. That I had to do something about it if I ever wanted to be accepted.

I cried so many times behind closed doors, hiding my shame where no one could see it. And in those dark, lonely moments, I made a promise to myself that I would never give them a reason to call me fat again. I would never be laughed at or ridiculed for the way I looked. I would force myself into their idea of acceptable, no matter what it took.

But I was just a child, desperate to fit into a world that made me feel like I didn't belong. I had no idea what fitness or health even meant. I only knew that I had to be smaller, that I had to erase everything they found offensive. I found pieces of my father's work equipment and tied them around my legs, forcing myself to do makeshift workouts. Crunches, squats — anything to burn away what they hated. Anything to punish myself for not being good enough.

It became an obsession, a ritual, and an act of self-destruction disguised as discipline. Food became the enemy, and hunger became my greatest accomplishment. I trained myself to survive on as little as possible, believing that the emptiness I felt was proof of progress. The less I ate, the more powerful I felt.

By the time I was a teenager, I had perfected the art of starvation. My daily routine was nothing but punishment. Breakfast was a single biscuit with a bit of cacao. Lunch, if I allowed myself to have it, was a few bites of whatever I could find. Dinner was forbidden. Every morning, I would step on the scale like it was a test of my worth. 47 kilograms. That number became my rule, and anything above it was failure. I still remember how I would go to sleep trembling every night, my body shaking uncontrollably from hunger, but I refused to let myself eat.

People around me praised my thinness, mistaking my sickness for strength. They called it discipline, dedication, and self-control. They complimented me for what I was doing to myself without ever understanding the heaviness underneath. One friend at university even said, *"It's not me who is your friend. Skeleton is your best friend."* And I believed her.

But the reality was, I wasn't in control . I was a prisoner of my own insecurities. The constant hunger, the endless cycle of self-hate, the war I made against my own body — it consumed everything. I was destroying myself from the inside out, thinking I was succeeding.

And that war didn't end in my teenage years, it followed me into adulthood — into my twenties, and well into my thirties.

When my father passed away in 2016, everything shifted. His death tore through me like nothing I had ever experienced. The grief was overwhelming, but it forced me to see the truth I had been avoiding for so long. My health deteriorated rapidly, my body finally breaking down from years of starvation and self-inflicted anorexia. I was diagnosed with multiple chronic digestive issues – many of them irreversible.

I looked in the mirror and saw what I had done to myself — every rib and vertebra visible, a body damaged by years of control and restriction. My digestive system was no longer functioning properly, and I knew some of that damage would stay with me forever. My mind felt equally depleted, worn down from years of pressure, harsh routines, and impossible expectations I had placed on myself. But more than anything, I was tired. Not just physically, but in a way that left no space for anything else. Tired of punishing myself, tired of carrying a constant sense of failure, tired of waking up each day already drained. I didn't stop because I had suddenly found peace. I stopped because I couldn't do it anymore. There was no more strength left to keep fighting a battle that had already taken too much from me.

I started eating. I let myself enjoy any kind of food without guilt or shame. I learned to see food as nourishment instead of the enemy. I joined a fitness club not to shrink myself but to strengthen myself. I found yoga and built routines that respected my body instead of breaking it.

Healing wasn't perfect. It didn't come easily, and it didn't fix everything, but it was a beginning I chose for myself.

Rebuilding my body also meant rebuilding my mind. The more I nourished my physical health, the stronger my mental resilience became. The more I allowed myself to heal, the more I realized how deeply intertwined my body and mind had always been. They had been suffering together, breaking together. And now, they were healing together.

It wasn't about erasing the past. It was about understanding that my physical and mental pain had been fighting the same battle all along. The wounds I caused my body were the same wounds I carved into my mind. Healing had to come from both places, or it wouldn't come at all.

Now, I choose health over punishment.

I choose nourishment over starvation.

I choose to honor my body and mind because they deserve to be cared for, respected, and strengthened.

What I have reclaimed is not just my physical health, but my mental freedom . I am no longer at war with myself.

I am whole.

And I am enough exactly as I am.

Becoming Unbreakable

Strength isn't what I once thought it was. It's not about being tough or fighting through everything with determination and force. It's not about how much you can carry or how well you can hold everything together. True strength begins the moment I choose to live in my truth — regardless of what anyone else expects of me.

I used to measure myself against standards that had nothing to do with who I was or what I wanted. I spent years chasing ideals that left me feeling restless and incomplete. I pushed myself through rigid routines that silenced my instincts. And that fulfillment that I've been chasing? It never came – because it was never about doing more. It was about doing what was true to me. It was about finding my own way.

My body was the first thing I had to rebuild. It had taken years of overtaking in the name of perfection — working out until I was drained, skipping meals when I felt I didn't deserve them, forcing myself into patterns that never felt natural.

When I finally let go of that mindset, something shifted. I started moving because it made me feel alive, not because I was trying to meet someone else's definition of beauty or strength. Yoga and stretching became about feeling connected to myself, about breathing and letting go instead of forcing and striving. Fitness became my source of renewal — a way to feel present and whole.

My body became my temple and something worthy of cherishing and protecting. I fed it with intention, with care, with kindness. I allowed myself to rest without guilt. I honored the signals my body gave me instead of silencing them for too long.

But the body was only the beginning. My mind had been trapped in patterns of self-judgment and criticism that I could barely recognize my own thoughts. I was constantly chasing someone else's definition of success, never pausing to ask myself if any of it truly mattered to me.

I had to unlearn everything that kept me trapped in cycles of doubt and fear. I had to question every belief I had accepted as truth, every story I had told myself about what I could or couldn't do. I realized that my mind had been working against me because I had been feeding it the wrong things for too long.

I chose to let go of the beliefs that kept me stuck. I replaced criticism with curiosity and impatience with acceptance . I began to feed my mind with thoughts that expanded me, with knowledge that felt genuine and true. I allowed myself to grow without the weight of proving anything to anyone.

But the deepest transformation happened when I finally paid attention to my own soul. The part of me that came alive in stillness, in nature, with animals, through writing. The part that didn't care how things looked, only how they felt. The part that didn't want to be more — it just wanted to be whole.

I began creating space for the things that brought me peace. Not the kind of peace that had to be earned, but the kind that already lived inside me, waiting for me to come back to it. I didn't need to prove anything. I didn't need to keep up. I just needed to be honest about what I truly needed — and give myself permission to have it.

That's where my strength came from. Not from control. Not from perfection. But from living in a way that felt steady and true. I started making decisions that matched who I was — even when they were difficult, even when they meant letting go of everything I had built around the wrong foundation.

Becoming unbreakable was never about reaching some perfect state of strength. It was about taking back everything I had lost, healing what needed to be healed, and building a life that felt like mine. It was about honoring myself enough to reject anything that didn't serve me, even when it was hard, even when it meant letting go of everything I once thought I couldn't live without.

You don't become unbreakable by proving something to the world.

You become unbreakable the moment you decide that your own life, your own peace, your own truth — are not up for negotiation ever again.

Choosing Yourself Every Day

Life begins to feel different when you stop abandoning yourself for the sake of being understood. When your peace becomes more important than explaining your choices, and when protecting your energy no longer feels like isolation but like freedom. You start to see the difference between connection and obligation, between being included and being valued, and between loyalty and neglecting your own truth. It's not a dramatic transformation. It's something deeper — the subtle but powerful shift.

I spent years overdelivering, overcompensating, and overextending myself — not because anyone asked me to, but because I hadn't yet realized I was enough without trying so hard. I became the one who held everything together, carried it all, and showed up no matter what — all because of fear. Fear of not being needed. Fear of being forgotten. Fear of being seen as less if I dared to need something for myself. I didn't know that worth didn't have to be earned through emptiness. I didn't know I was allowed to belong to myself first.

What transformed wasn't my ability to love others — it was my willingness to include myself in that love. I started asking different questions. Instead of *"How do I make this work?"* I asked, *"Does this feel good to me?"* Instead of *"How do I keep the peace?"* I asked, *"What is it costing me?"* I stopped betraying my instincts just to avoid disappointing people. I stopped holding onto things that left me feeling smaller. And when I did, I discovered a version of me that had been there all along — the one who didn't need to earn love by trying so hard.

This chapter of my life has been about honoring what's real. I no longer feel drawn to chaos disguised as connection, or surface-level conversations that go nowhere. I crave honesty, depth, stillness, and the kind of respect that doesn't ask me to be less in order to be accepted. I have stopped trying to meet timelines that were never mine. I no longer measure my value through comparison. I've let go of the pressure to arrive anywhere quickly because I understand now that presence is more powerful than arrival. There's no destination more important than the relationship I have with myself.

Writing this book has not been about telling people how to live — it's been about remembering how to live fully, about coming home to myself in the small, conscious ways I chose to stop abandoning my own needs. Every word was a mirror, and through it, I met parts of myself I had forgotten I even missed. This wasn't about healing for a perfect ending. It was about healing for a peaceful beginning.

Choosing yourself every day is not a one-time act. It's a lifelong commitment to no longer participate in what depletes you. It's the promise to walk away when staying means disconnecting from your own needs. It's the courage to love yourself in moments when you feel unlovable. It's the steady reminder that you are not here to perform, to prove, or to perfect — you are here to live.

And so I choose myself. Not because I have mastered every lesson, not because I always feel brave or know exactly what comes next, but because I now understand the cost of not choosing myself — the weight of silence, the exhaustion of abandoning my own wellbeing, the ache of constantly shrinking to make others more comfortable. I've lived through what it means to give too much and ask too little in return. I've felt the emptiness of being surrounded but unseen, needed but not nurtured, loved conditionally but never truly met.

And I have no desire to live like that ever again.

Choosing myself means I've stopped waiting for others to tell me I'm enough because I've finally stopped asking questions to which I already know the answer. It means I no longer explain my boundaries, soften my truth to keep the peace, or sit in rooms where my voice must be diluted to be heard. It means that I wake up each day and honor the woman I have fought to become — the one who didn't give up on herself, even when she felt invisible, even when no one rooted for her healing, even when no one noticed she was breaking and rebuilding at the same time.

It means I will continue to walk through this life with my heart open and my standards high, with my energy guarded and my spirit intact. I will pour into people who pour back, I will protect my softness without apologizing for it, and I will say no without guilt and yes without fear. That I will trust my timing, even when it's slower than expected, and my path, even when it doesn't look like anyone else's.

I no longer need to be everything for everyone. I just need to be everything for me. And that is not selfish — that is sacred.

This isn't the end of a chapter — it's the return to the beginning.

The beginning of living as I am, not as I was told to be.

The beginning of taking up space, and belonging here exactly as I am.

The beginning of loving myself in action, not theory.

The beginning of honoring my voice, even if it shakes, my needs even if they're misunderstood, and my growth even when it's inconvenient for others.

Because if I've learned anything, it's that the deepest form of love is not what we receive from others — it's the unwavering decision to stand beside ourselves through it all. That kind of love doesn't come from being chosen. It comes from choosing.

And I've finally chosen myself — fully, deeply, completely — without delay, without conditions, without looking back.

And now that I have, I truly feel free — not because anything changed, but because I did.

THE SHIFT

The Sacred Return

Each day, you choose yourself — not by saying it, but by showing it. In the way you move, the way you care for your space, the way you create small moments that remind you that your life belongs to you.

This shift is not about protecting your energy. That chapter has already passed. This is about cultivating it — nourishing it through the small, personal rituals that remind you every day: this is your life now. Not a life you're escaping from. Not a life you're managing. But a life that feels like home.

Each day, you make space for one grounding experience that brings you back to yourself — not because you're trying to heal, but because it feels good to be present in your body, alive in your senses, and rooted in the life you've chosen to live.

This isn't a checklist or a fixed routine. It's a rhythm, a feeling, and a way you return.

- Some days, it might be fifteen minutes of gentle stretching or yoga — not to change your body, but to feel it from the inside.
- Other days, it's being on the beach, barefoot, breathing in the salt air, letting your body soften into stillness.
- Maybe it's taking the time to massage your legs, your neck, your arms — not because they hurt, but because they carry you.
- Or stepping into a warm shower and simply placing your hands on your heart and stomach, noticing how far you've come

without needing to say a word.
- Sometimes, it's lighting a candle in the evening — not for ambiance, but as a way of closing the day with intention, telling yourself: this time is mine now.

Whatever form it takes, you do it with care. Not urgency. And you repeat it — not because you have to, but because it reminds you who you are when the noise fades away.

This is not a temporary act of self-care.

This is a life built on self-respect.

This is your sacred return — not once, but every day, you choose to live by your ultimate standard: peace within your body, clarity within your mind, and a life that feels fully lived from within.

She rose – not to be seen, but because she finally saw herself.

Epilogue

The most important decision we ever make is to stop suffering. Not because life stops being difficult, but because we choose not to keep living inside the pain that already happened. We decide to seek joy, even when things don't go our way. We stop waiting for peace to arrive after everything is fixed and instead start creating it right here, inside the imperfect, because that's where life really happens.

Nothing in this world is forever — not the ache, fear, or even the pain that once felt unbearable. Everything passes. Slowly. Unevenly. If we let it. Healing doesn't come all at once. It comes in moments so small that they almost go unnoticed. In a breath we didn't know we were holding. In the sudden peace of not reacting the way we used to.

The days we forget to laugh are the ones we lose the most because laughter is life, reminding us that we are still alive. That even after everything, something inside us still longs for joy.

But to feel like that again, something in us needs to begin to heal. And healing often starts when we feel at ease, safe enough to let go.

The greatest healers are not always found in hospitals.

They live in the sun's warmth, reminding us we're still here.

In the love of family – the kind that makes you forget the world outside and remember what truly matters.

In the peace of animals who sit beside us without asking anything in return.

In the ease of nature that lets us be exactly as we are.

In the beauty of travel that resets what life made heavy.

The freedom of the ocean makes us feel light again.

In the strength of a body that is able to move.

In the comfort of food that feels like kindness, not control.

In the decision to put yourself first, without apology.

And in the kind of love that makes you feel safe, not small.

When you live by these truths, you begin to find something most people spend their lives chasing – not more, not better – but peace in the now.

And not only outside, but also in how you see yourself. And when you stand in front of the mirror, don't rush past. Stay. Even if your face has changed. Even if the years have drawn lines you didn't ask for. Stay. Because the person looking back is someone who made it through. A person who gave everything and kept going. Who felt pain and still chose love. Who lost so much, but never lost themselves.

You don't need to become someone else. You need to remember who you are — someone who kept walking without directions. Someone who now deserves to rest without guilt. Someone who is still here, despite it all.

We're all just passing through this life. None of this — not the bodies we have, the places we stand, or the people we hold — is forever. So take the longer way if it brings more light. Say what matters while you still can. Let your body move because it can. Laugh until your face hurts. Cry when you need to. And love — not when it's easy, but when it's true.

This life was never meant to be flawless. It was meant to be felt because it is precious, and it doesn't wait.

And if you've made it here — to this breath, this page, then you already know:

You are not who the world told you to be.

You are who you choose to become.

And you are — finally, fully — the version of you that was always meant to be.

Acknowledgments

To **Sarah,** thank you for believing in this story and guiding it into the world with care and integrity. Your support through the design, editing, formatting, and publishing process made all the difference.

To **Liu Jo**, for styling me in a way that felt both powerful and true to who I am — your vision helped bring this moment to life.

To **Gerald and the Stu Studios**– thank you for capturing not just images but emotion, energy, and truth. Your work reflects everything this book stands for.

To **Nermine**, for your artistry and care in creating a hairstyle that made me feel elegant, strong, and myself.

To **Rana**, for the makeup that enhanced, not masked, and for your presence on a day that meant so much.

To **Elena** and **The Loft Avenue team**, for pampering me with warmth and attention to every detail — your care made me feel held, relaxed, and truly myself.

To **Ali** — the brilliant mind behind my website, social media, and the illustrations that brought this book to life visually. Your incredible talent, dedication, and support made this dream feel complete.

To **everyone else who contributed** — in ways big or small — to bringing this book to life: thank you. Whether through your words, your time, your energy, or simply your belief in me, your presence is felt on every page.

Each of you, in your own way, helped me step fully into this chapter — not just as a writer but as the woman I've become.

In Loving Memory of Ariel

October 2009 – June 2025

My beloved poodle, my forever friend.

For sixteen years, you stood by my side —
across two continents, through every storm, through every chapter.

You loved without asking.
You stayed without question.
And in the hardest season of my healing,
you gave me your last breath.

You were more than words could ever hold —
and I hope these pages carry the unconditional love you gave me…
and the unconditional love I will always have for you.

Run free now, my boy.
My heart will always run with you.

INDEX

A

Abandonment: In relationships 19
Abandoned: Emotional abandonment 24, 90
Acceptance: 27, 116, 132

B

Belonging: 27, 101, 105, 136
Body: Healing through movement 66, 90, 99
Body: Relationship with 22, 23, 37, 52
Body: Trauma and memory storage 67, 82, 127
Boundaries: Emotional 89, 121, 136
Boundaries: Setting and maintaining 36, 40, 115
Boundaries: With self and others 44, 76, 121

C

Childhood: Emotional neglect 22, 38, 45
Childhood: Responsibilities 38
Childhood: Trauma 22, 35, 55, 81
Comparison: Social media and image 97, 99, 102, 135
Control: Illusion of control 52, 53, 55, 127
Control: Letting go of 56, 89

D

Discipline: Beyond motivation 18, 23
Discipline: Consistency and values 35, 52, 65, 76
Discipline: Emotional resilience 22, 66
Disconnect: From self 18, 135

E

Energy: Emotional drain 39, 73, 112
Energy: Reclaiming and protecting 43, 106, 114, 121, 134, 136, 138
Expectations: Overcoming external pressure 26, 27
Expectations: Societal and familial 17, 25, 35, 103

F

Fear: Of not being seen 17, 33, 42
Fear: Of being forgotten 27, 41, 134
Freedom: Choosing peace 36, 120, 131
Freedom: Mental and spiritual 41, 75

G

Gratitude 116
Growth: Personal transformation 73, 137
Growth: Through adversity 75, 89

H

Healing: After betrayal and trauma 39
Healing: Self-led recovery 56, 135, 142
Healing: Non-linear journey 130
Healing: Process and setbacks 58, 83

I

Integrity: As resilience 74

L

Letting go: Emotional baggage 56, 58, 132
Letting go: Past pain and stories 25, 57
Letting go: Relationships 133
Love: Conditional vs. unconditional love 21, 26, 33
Love: Safe vs. toxic love 21, 136
Love: Self-love 36

M

Mastery: Ownership of life 72, 75
Mental clutter: Overthinking and emotional noise 54
Motivation: Replaced by discipline 69, 76
Motivation: Unreliable source 67, 77

P

Pain: As teacher 37, 69, 84
Pain: As transformation 39, 73, 82
Pain: Physical and emotional · 25, 35, 66
Presence: Living in the now 42, 57
Presence: Mindfulness in daily life 59, 89

R

Relationships: People pleasing 35, 38
Relationships: Real connection 42, 112
Relationships: Toxic dynamics 35, 36, 69

S

Self-Abandonment: 24, 36, 37, 46, 134
Self-Respect: Daily choices that honor self 40, 42, 57
Self-Respect: Rebuilding from within 37, 58, 75
Self-Worth: 42, 103
Social Media: Image distortion 97, 100

V

Values: Integrity over impulse 77, 86

W

Wounds: Breaking cycles 54, 56

www.ingramcontent.com/pod-product-compliance
Lightning Source LLC
Chambersburg PA
CBHW060157050426
42446CB00013B/2875